COMPASSIONATE
SOLDIER

Another Shadow Mountain book
by Jerry Borrowman

Beyond the Call of Duty

COMPASSIONATE
SOLDIER

REMARKABLE **TRUE STORIES**
OF MERCY, HEROISM, AND HONOR
FROM THE BATTLEFIELD

JERRY BORROWMAN

SHADOW
MOUNTAIN

Visit us at ShadowMountain.com

Library of Congress Cataloging-in-Publication Data

Names: Borrowman, Jerry, author.
Title: Compassionate soldier : remarkable true stories of mercy, heroism, and honor from the battlefield.
Description: Salt Lake City, Utah : Shadow Mountain, [2017] | Includes bibliographical references and index.
Identifiers: LCCN 2016048519 (print) | ISBN 9781629722924 (hardbound : alk. paper) | ISBN 9781629735191 (ebook)
Subjects: LCSH: War—Moral and ethical aspects. | Compassion—Anecdotes. | Courage—Anecdotes. | Soldiers—Anecdotes. | LCGFT: Biographies. | Anecdotes.
Classification: LCC U22 .B63 2017 | DDC 355.0092/2—dc23
LC record available at https://lccn.loc.gov/2016048519

Printed in the United States of America
Publishers Printing

10 9 8 7 6 5 4 3 2 1

Patriotism is not enough.
I must have no hatred or
bitterness for anyone.

EDITH CAVELL

CONTENTS

INTRODUCTION

Imagine you are on the battlefield and in the throes of fighting a war. Your chance of survival is uncertain. Suddenly, you find yourself with a crucial decision to make—you have the opportunity to save someone's life, but trying to do so may put you in harm's way. Do you risk your life to help save another's?

How often do we think about the welfare of others before our own? The dictionary defines *compassion* as "a feeling of deep sympathy and sorrow for another who is stricken by misfortune, accompanied by a strong desire to alleviate the suffering."

In war, compassion also requires courage. That is why, in a situation where cruelty is the norm, compassion is so unexpected. Soldiers are taught to disregard the humanity of the enemy so they can act against them. When individuals act generously for someone who is in danger, even at the risk of their own life, such actions are noteworthy and inspiring.

The following remarkable true stories show that a real hero is a compassionate one. We may never be a soldier on a battlefield, but every day we are offered choices: to be kind or unkind, to show love or ignore someone who needs our help, to forget ourselves or live selfishly.

Compassionate Soldier honors brave men and women who showed compassion when it was not expected or required. In most cases, this compassion created peril for the ones who offered it, but they proceeded in spite of the risk. In all these situations, it is humbling to witness their actions, even from a distance, because the question inevitably arises, "Would I have behaved as well as they did?" Perhaps that is the most important trait of real heroes—their ability to inspire the rest of us to do a little better.

PART ONE

COMPASSION ON THE BATTLEFIELD

CHAPTER 1

CAPTAIN FERGUSON AND GENERAL WASHINGTON

THE LAW OF ARMS

Unknown to General George Washington and his aide, the three British sharpshooters who had them in their sights carried the new Ferguson rifle. The most accurate weapon in the world, it could hit its target within three hundred yards. General Washington was less than one hundred yards away.

So why did the British officer order his men to lower their weapons?

That British officer was Captain Patrick Ferguson of the British 70th Light Foot Regiment. He was a professional soldier in His Majesty's Army and, like most other officers, had purchased his captain's commission as a way to advance in rank, status, and pay. A British-trained soldier and a man of honor, he was deeply offended by the American rebels' use of guerrilla war tactics.[1] Ferguson believed that gentlemen always faced each other on an open field in combat.

In contrast, the Americans believed in the element of surprise, often concealing themselves behind trees and foliage, waiting to attack the enemy. It was not uncommon for the patriots, as the colonists called themselves, to fire on British troops from behind. After killing a few soldiers, the patriots would slip into the woods beyond the reach of return fire. This intermittent harassment increased the anxiety felt by British troops because they never knew when or where to expect an attack.

CAPTAIN PATRICK FERGUSON

Patrick Ferguson was a remarkable man. Born in Scotland, he was the second son in an influential family. His father was a judge, and his older brother a member of Parliament. Pattie, as the family called him, joined the British army at age fifteen. First assigned to the Royal North British Dragoons, he served in Germany and Flanders in the Seven Years War.

As the European war was ending, he volunteered for service in the Caribbean Islands, nicknamed the "fever islands." Most Britons who served there suffered from the heat and from insect-borne diseases. Ferguson, on the other hand, thrived in the unfamiliar climate. He wrote home:

> All West India Climates are alike to me, & actually seem to improve my Constitution. I have been in five Different Islands & have enjoyed uncommon good health in them all: I cannot however say that our men so are healthy as at home, owing I am convinced to the necessity they are under of eating Salt provisions & the Excesses they are apt to indulge themselves in with new rum, which is the only kind they can well Afford to purchase. The Officers, however, are as healthy as can be imagined.[2]

While a commanding officer in the Caribbean, Ferguson hoped to make his fortune by purchasing land there and operating a plantation. But he quickly became bored with that kind of life and turned his business over to his younger brother.

INVENTOR

Returning to Britain, Ferguson worked hard to improve his military prowess, particularly his skill in handling rifles. In fact, so great was his talent that he started making improvements to the breech-loading rifle that was used by sportsman. His goal was to turn it into a military weapon.

Ferguson's incremental changes made for a highly improved weapon. For example, he reduced the number of turns of the ramrod needed to seal the barrel for firing when loading powder and shot through the breech (the back end of the barrel) instead of the muzzle. This change allowed him to get off more shots in faster succession. He also developed a method to quickly clean the barrel of fouled powder and ball, which could mean the difference between life and death for a soldier who was effectively out of action while preparing his next shot.

All of these improvements were significant. In a demonstration before his superiors, Ferguson cleared the rifle barrel of wet powder and fired a second shot in less than thirty seconds. By comparison, a fouled muzzleloader could take more than half an hour to clean and require help from more than one soldier to pry out the ball and wet powder.

An observer at the demonstration said about Ferguson and his rifle:

> In June 1776, he gave a demonstration at Woolwich before Lord Amherst, Viscount Townshend, General Harvey, and several other prominent officers. He astonished the beholders. "Notwithstanding

a heavy rain and high wind, he fired," according to a contemporary, ". . . after the rate of four shots per minute at a target two hundred yards distant. He next fired six shots in one minute. . . . He then poured a bottle of water into the pan and barrel of the piece when loaded, so as to wet every grain of powder; and in less than half a minute, he fired with her, as well as ever, without extracting the ball. Lastly, he hit the bull's eye, lying on his back on the ground. Incredible as it may seem to many, considering the variation of the wind, and wetness of the weather, he only missed the target three times, during the whole course of the experiment."[3]

Ferguson's breechloader was remarkable in being accurate to three hundred yards—the equivalent of the length of three modern football fields. Muzzle loaders were accurate from only fifty to one hundred yards. That Ferguson could place a pattern of shots close to each other from hundreds of yards away showed his skill as a marksman as well.

He sought patents on his accumulated changes to the standard breechloader and engaged Britain's foremost arms maker, a Swiss man named Durs Egg, to produce his rifles. Ferguson's family benefited from the sale of Ferguson rifles for many years after his death.

THE REVOLUTIONARY WAR

In addition to his skills in soldiering and inventing, Patrick Ferguson was a great writer. His letters to his family are filled with wry historical insights, and he was among a handful of soldiers who wrote for *The Royal Gazette,* a newspaper published in British-occupied New York City during the Revolutionary War. His essays were earnest and appealing in their attempt to maintain the morale of loyalists and British soldiers. And he also tried to persuade wavering patriots to return their loyalty to Britain.

What many Americans today may not realize is that the colonists were divided about whether or not to break with Britain. It is estimated that just one-third of the people were avid patriots, another third were loyal to the Crown, and the remaining third were indifferent. This third group often switched loyalties during the war, siding with whichever group was nearest.

It was to this last group that Ferguson made direct appeals to cease their folly and return their loyalties to the king. Like most British officers in America at the time, he believed that once the rebellion died down, the colonists would realize all the benefits of belonging to a great empire, which they had lost by separating from the mother country, and would plead to be taken back by the Crown.

To drive this idea into their hearts, he wrote under the name John Bull a particularly satirical piece expounding the wondrous blessings Americans had compared to their European counterparts. He asked why they chose to put their good fortune at risk when Britain was such a benevolent parent. John Bull was a symbol of Great Britain (something like Uncle Sam), who was portrayed as an English country gentleman, full of common sense and good will.

The character of the fictional John Bull was different from Ferguson's, however. Ferguson was intense, a zealot tirelessly pushing his men to destroy the revolutionary cause. In his public writings, he often reminded Americans that if the king decided to punish the rebels by burning their towns and crops, the British could easily force the rebels to their knees. But, he reminded his readers, because the American colonies were still a Crown possession and because at least one-third of the people were loyal to the king, the British army had shown extreme forbearance to the rebels in their prosecution of the war. Many readers of Ferguson's articles interpreted his warnings as a veiled threat that if the patriots didn't soon concede, the harsh tactics used so frequently in European wars would be turned against them.

FERGUSON SAVES GEORGE WASHINGTON

The thing that made Ferguson the most indignant was the Americans' refusal to fight by the accepted rules of engagement on an open field. He was proud of his profession and felt that the rebels were trampling on time-honored virtues of fair play by using uncultivated terrain to their advantage.

At Brandywine Creek, Ferguson sent three men forward to shoot two unidentified rebel soldiers on horseback. He changed his mind when the Americans rode past, and he ordered his soldiers not to fire on them from behind.

Still curious, however, Ferguson moved forward to see the two enemy soldiers for himself. Here is what he later wrote about the encounter (original spelling):

> We had not layn long when a Rebell Officer [in] a Huzzar Dress passed . . . our Army within 100 yards of my right flank, not perceiving us—he was followed by another dressed in dark green on blue mounted on a very good bay horse with a remarkable large high cocked hat. I ordered three good shots to . . . fire at them but the idea disgusted me and I recalled them. The Huzzar in returning made a Circuit, but the other passed within 100 yards of us, upon which I advanced from the wood towards him; Upon my calling he stopd, but after looking at me proceeded. I again drew his attention and made signs to him to Stop, levelling my piece at him; but he slowly continued his way.
>
> The day after I had Just been telling this Story to some wounded Officers, . . . when one of our surgeons . . . came in and told us that [some Rebel officers] had been informing him that General Washington was

all morning with the Light Troops generally in their front and only attended by a French Officer in a huzzar dress he himself mounted and dressed as above described; the oddness of their dress had puzzled me and made me take notice of it. I am not sorry that I did not know all the time who it was.[4]

Ferguson made it clear later that even had he known the American officer's identity, he would *not* have shot the soldiers in the back. Ferguson's sense of honor did not permit such a breach of military etiquette.

It is interesting, even puzzling, to note from Ferguson's account that Washington rode away slowly when Ferguson challenged him. Perhaps General Washington felt he was out of range, not knowing how accurate the new British guns were at such a distance. Or perhaps he expected gentlemanly behavior from a British officer. At any rate, Ferguson could easily have killed Washington had he chosen to violate his own principles.

A part of the story that is not often told is that just moments after he allowed Washington to pass out of sight, Ferguson was shot by an American sharpshooter who did not share his sense of battlefield etiquette. The pain of his shattered right elbow was incredible. He was transferred to Philadelphia, where during the next eight months he endured, without anesthetic, multiple operations to remove bone splinters from his arm.

Even in this adversity, however, he maintained his good humor, writing home to his family that there was an ongoing debate about whether he ought to be allowed to keep his arm or whether it should be amputated and "turned over to the worms."[5]

A FIGHTER UNTIL THE END

His right arm permanently disabled, Ferguson learned to write, shoot, and handle his rifle with his left. Then he returned to active duty. Not long afterward, his troops attacked at daybreak a sleeping enemy force under the command of Lieutenant Colonel Carl von Bose. They used bayonets in the grisly affair.

Ferguson expressed his dismay at the Americans' failure to post lookouts so the rebel troops could have put up a better defense. He also reported that he spared three houses used by patriot soldiers, even though it was to his advantage to destroy the buildings. His reason? The homes were owned by innocent Quakers with whom he had no quarrel.[6]

In time, Patrick Ferguson was promoted to major and appointed inspector of militia in South Carolina. He was assigned to train loyalist troops to fight to keep the Carolinas a part of the British empire. The British and their loyalist allies were often successful in these battles, eventually capturing Charlotte, North Carolina.

But the patriots were not subdued. Using guerrilla war tactics, they took vengeance on a contingent of loyalists at the battle of Musgrove's Mill. Ferguson was dispatched with loyalist militia to pursue the retreating rebels.

This pursuit led to the battle of King's Mountain, in which Ferguson and his loyalists were outnumbered. Standing upright in his stirrups and leading a charge, the British major was shot from his horse. When a rebel approached him to accept his surrender, Ferguson shot him. Enraged patriot soldiers in return shot him to death. His body desecrated by angry American troops, Ferguson was buried under a cairn (a pile of stones) on King's Mountain. Today, a monument marks his grave.

Patrick Ferguson is remembered for his skill as a leader, a marksman, and an inventor. He is also known as the man who could have killed George Washington but whose honor forbade him to shoot a man in the back. We owe him gratitude for his integrity.

CHAPTER 2

RICHARD KIRKLAND

ANGEL AT THE BATTLE OF FREDERICKSBURG

The American War Between the States was a brutal affair. Weaponry had improved significantly in the eighty years since the Revolutionary War, but no corresponding improvements had been made in treatment for wounds and injuries. With more than 620,000 dead and 400,000 wounded, the Civil War is still the costliest war in American history in terms of soldiers injured and killed.

The War Between the States is unique in that it was a war of ideology rather than geographical conquest. To the North, the Confederate states were still a part of the Union but in rebellion. To the South, the war was about seceding from the Union in order to hold onto a way of life being squeezed to death by the political establishment in the North. In 1862, after nearly a year of war, the conflict crystallized as a struggle over slavery when Abraham Lincoln issued the Emancipation Proclamation, which freed the slaves in rebel-held territory. Not everyone supported this new objective, in either the North or the South. What is certain is that the Civil War was the only war in our history that pitted neighbor against neighbor, brother against brother, and former comrades in arms against one another.

A most disastrous campaign of the war for the Union was the battle of Fredericksburg in Virginia. Federal forces made several attempts to take a well-fortified position on the Confederate side of the Rappahannock River. These assaults led to a staggering loss of life and heart-wrenching suffering during the attack on Marye's Heights in December 1832. Failing to change tactics once they recognized the strength of the Confederate position, Union generals continued to send wave after wave of soldiers into a killing mill. Thousands were killed or wounded.

The battle stretched on for two days. During the fighting, wounded Federal soldiers lay unattended in a mountain of corpses where they spent a miserable Saturday night in freezing weather, unable to move to safety. As Sunday dawned and more failed assaults took place, the Union wounded became increasingly desperate for aid. In this awful setting, an act of mercy by a Confederate soldier, Sergeant Richard R. Kirkland, earned him the gratitude of dying Union soldiers and brought the raging battle to a temporary halt.

CHOOSING THE RIGHT LEADERS

The War Between the States started in April 1861 with the shelling of Fort Sumter at Charleston, South Carolina. Officers in the various branches of the United States military were forced to choose sides in this conflict—a wrenching decision for many of them, who had served side by side in previous military campaigns.

General Robert E. Lee is a good example of one who had to choose between conflicting loyalties. He was easily one of the most successful officers in the United States Army, having distinguished himself in military service for more than three decades. On the eve of the Civil War, Lee was superintendent of the United States Military Academy at West Point in upstate New York. He trained many officers who later served on opposing sides.

Lee's military prowess led to an invitation from the newly elected United States president, Abraham Lincoln, to take command of the Army of the Potomac, the most senior military post there was. But though Lee felt that secession was wrong, he considered himself a Virginian first. With a heavy heart, he declined the Union appointment when Virginia seceded. Lee thus became an enemy of the country whose Constitution he had sworn to uphold.

During the first years of the war, Lee was able to stymie the North, inflicting defeat after defeat on a succession of Union generals. And he did so with fewer troops and less equipment.

In 1862, Lee was given command of the Army of Northern Virginia, the premier fighting unit of the Confederacy. This promotion took him to the battle of Fredericksburg, where he inflicted a punishing defeat on Union forces.

Abraham Lincoln, as commander-in-chief of the United States military forces, had a difficult time finding generals who could inspire their men in battle. This frustrating state of affairs continued until 1864, when he finally found in Ulysses S. Grant the fighting general he was looking for. Only then were Federal forces able to capitalize on their overwhelming numerical superiority and the astonishing industrial output of the northern states.

But in November 1862, Lincoln's problems with his generals were not yet resolved, even when General Ambrose Burnside was appointed commanding general of the Army of the Potomac.

THE BATTLE ENDS

Despite the futility of continued assaults on Marye's Heights, General Burnside became obsessed with winning the battle. He ordered his generals to mount more attacks. Finally they convinced him that further assaults were hopeless. Burnside gave in to despair and allowed his army to retreat to the Union side of the Rappahannock River.

When the Federal troops finally withdrew, General Lee called a temporary truce so that ambulances could evacuate the wounded to field hospitals. He also allowed Union soldiers time to bury their comrades who had died in battle.

Burnside's defeat was complete, and Lee's victory added to his reputation for invincibility, in both the South and the North. Lee had smashed Lincoln's hopes for victory against the double stone wall and sunken road of Marye's Heights.

The statistics at Fredericksburg are grim: 114,000 Union soldiers faced off against 72,000 Confederates. At the end of the battle, the Union had suffered 1,284 dead, 9,600 wounded, and 1,769 taken prisoner or missing. The losses of Lee's Army of Northern Virginia were less than half those numbers, with 608 dead, 4,116 wounded, and 653 captured or missing.

General Burnside withdrew to Washington, D.C., angry and discouraged. He blamed the generals under his command for his failures in the battle, even though the task he had given them was hopeless. Lincoln reluctantly accepted Burnside's plans for a new campaign upstream from Fredericksburg in January 1863.

But winter proved a greater foe of the Union than the Confederate army. Torrential rains and snows turned the approaches to the Rappahannock into impassable mud that bogged down wagons and artillery, exhausting men and horses before they even reached the battlefield. Burnside resigned his command in the face of this second failure.

FREDERICKSBURG

Fredericksburg, bordered on two sides by the Rappahannock River, is situated about halfway between Washington, D.C., and Richmond, Virginia, the capital of the Confederacy. This location gave it military significance far greater than the modest population of 5,000 residents would otherwise have deserved. In the course of the war, this venerable Southern town was occupied by Federal soldiers four different times.

In December 1862, Fredericksburg became the site of one of the bloodiest battles of the conflict. Because Washington, D.C., was so close to Confederate lines, the defense of the capital city was crucial for the North. Accordingly, the Army of the Potomac received the first call on men and equipment. Despite suffering defeat in the first battle of Fredericksburg, Lincoln still needed to expand the protective perimeter around Washington. Hence, a second attack on Fredericksburg would be undertaken in January 1863.

The fortunes of the Union in these battles turned mainly on the superb leadership of Robert E. Lee and the ineffective command of Ambrose Burnside. Lincoln wanted someone to seize the initiative, but insisting Burnside take action in the early winter turned out to be a serious mistake. Lincoln's desire for a year-end victory fell apart in the slaughter at the first battle of Fredericksburg.

A STONE WALL, A SUNKEN ROAD, AN INVITATION TO HORROR

The Maryes, a family prominent in Virginia, owned a large home atop a hill at one end of Fredericksburg. Lee could see from his reconnaissance of the area that the Union army would have to storm Marye's Heights to secure the town. He could also see that it would be virtually impossible for Federal forces to breach the double line of stone walls at the base of the hill on which the home sat. Lee positioned his best sharpshooters behind the inner wall, four men deep. He believed that if Union troops stormed the hill, the Confederates could shoot them down with little personal risk.

Five failed Union assaults validated Lee's belief. The assaults occurred on a blood-soaked Saturday and Sunday, December 12 and 13, 1862. Nearly 1,000 Federal troops were killed, their bodies forming an increasing mound that had to be climbed over by the next unfortunate group of attackers. Wounded Union soldiers were left behind at the failure of each attack, fully exposed to enemy gunfire and unable to return to the safety of their lines.

> These wretched men lay crying, groaning, and begging for water and help in the most agonizing manner, and we were unable to rescue them. . . . The rustle of a leaf or the cracking of a twig might send a shower of Rebel bullets into our ranks.—John Haley of the 17th Maine.[1]

At the height of the battle, more than 5,000 injured soldiers lay among the heaps of Union dead, where they were left to suffer from their wounds in the December cold. On Saturday evening, Federal soldiers crouching behind their lines listened in distress to the terrible sounds of suffering coming from the battlefield. A few ventured out under cover of darkness to offer comfort. Lieutenant Colonel Joshua Chamberlain of the 20th Maine recalled that he and a comrade spent most of the night lying between two dead soldiers to try to stay warm. When the cries of suffering overwhelmed them, he and his friend left the relative safety of their position to offer aid:

> We did what we could, but how little it was on a field so boundless for feeble human reach! Our best was to search the canteens of the dead for a draft of water for the dying; or to ease the posture of a broken limb; or to compress a severed artery of fast-ebbing life that might perhaps so be saved, with what little skill

we had been taught by our surgeons early in learning the tactics of saving as well as of destroying men. It was a place and time for farewells. Many a word was taken for far-away homes that otherwise might never have had one token from the field of the lost. It was something even to let the passing spirit know that its worth was not forgotten here.[2]

As Sunday morning dawned cold and foggy, the agonized cries of the wounded grew more desperate. Watching from behind the stone walls, Confederate sergeant Richard Kirkland of the Second South Carolina Volunteers listened to these cries for help with increasing anxiety. Finally, he could stand it no longer. Here is the firsthand account that General J. B. Kershaw of the Confederate army published in the *Charleston News & Courier*. He speaks of himself as "the General":

> All day those wounded men rent the air with their groans and agonizing cries of "Water! Water!"
>
> In the afternoon the General sat in the north room, upstairs, of Mrs. Stevens' house, in front of the road, surveying the field, when Kirkland came up. With an expression of indignant remonstrance pervading his person, his manner and the tone of his voice, he said: "General! I can't stand this."
>
> "What is the matter, Sergeant?" asked the General.
>
> He replied, "All night and all day I have heard those poor people crying for water, and I can stand it no longer. I come to ask permission to go and give them water."
>
> The General regarded him for a moment with feelings of profound admiration, and said: "Kirkland, don't you know that you would get a bullet through your head the moment you stepped over the wall?"

"Yes, sir," he said, "I know that; but if you will let me, I am willing to try it."

After a pause, the General said, "Kirkland, I ought not to allow you to run a risk, but the sentiment which actuates you is so noble that I will not refuse your request, trusting that God may protect you. You may go."

The Sergeant's eye lighted up with pleasure. He said, "Thank you, sir," and ran rapidly down stairs. . . .

With profound anxiety [the General] watched as [Kirkland] stepped over the wall on his errand of mercy—Christ-like mercy. Unharmed he reached the nearest sufferer. He knelt beside him, tenderly raised the drooping head, rested it gently upon his own noble breast, and poured the precious life-giving fluid down the fever scorched throat. This done, he laid him tenderly down, placed his knapsack under his head, straightened out his broken limb, spread his overcoat over him, replaced his empty canteen with a full one, and turned to another sufferer. By this time his purpose was well understood on both sides, and all danger was over.

From all parts of the field arose fresh cries of "Water, water; for God's sake, water!" More piteous still the mute appeal of some who could only feebly lift a hand to say, here, too, is life and suffering.

For an hour and a half did this ministering angel pursue his labor of mercy, nor ceased to go and return until he relieved all the wounded on that part of the field. He returned to his post wholly unhurt. Who shall say how sweet his rest that winter's night beneath the cold stars![3]

Many accounts, both Union and Confederate, were recorded of Sergeant Kirkland's bravery that day. They all indicate that when this young man, in his early twenties, first climbed up onto the outer wall with as many canteens of water slung over his shoulder as he could carry, the Union soldiers were so startled that they paused in their firing. When they realized what he was doing, the entire battlefield fell silent. A spontaneous shout of encouragement erupted as both Confederate and Federal soldiers cheered him on. Kirkland seemed not to notice. He was focused entirely on his mission of mercy.

When Kirkland's first group of canteens was empty, he disappeared back over the stone wall, and firing resumed on both sides. But when he stuck his head up a second time, the battlefield again went quiet while he went out to another group of wounded. This pattern continued for more than an hour and a half until virtually all the wounded were cared for.

A LASTING TRIBUTE

In his report of Kirkland's heroic acts, General Kershaw concluded:

> Little remains to be told. Sergeant Kirkland distinguished himself in battle at Gettysburg, and was promoted lieutenant. At Chickamauga he fell on the field of battle, in the hour of victory. He was but a youth when called away, and had never formed those ties from which might have resulted in a posterity to enjoy his fame and bless his country; but he has bequeathed to the American youth—yea, to the world—an example which dignifies our common humanity.

In the midst of the fury and folly of the battle of Fredericksburg, Sergeant Kirkland's act of heroism stands out because he was willing to risk his life to offer aid to the afflicted enemy. As his acts of kindness became known, his courage was celebrated in both Northern and Southern states, who knew him as the angel of Marye's Heights.

He continued his service to the Confederacy until, as noted by General Kershaw, losing his life at the Battle of Chickamauga on September 20, 1863. His body was laid to rest in Camden, South Carolina.

Today, a number of memorials pay tribute to Kirkland, including a bronze monument at the foot of Marye's Hill depicting Kirkland kneeling as he gives water to a wounded Union soldier. There is also an inscription on the wall of a memorial church in Gettysburg, Pennsylvania. In addition to these two monuments, people in both the North and South raised money to place a large stone slab over his grave in South Carolina commemorating his action.[4]

Thus, a young man who otherwise would have remained unknown to history found immortality because of his courage and humanity. In doing so, he fulfilled the charge given by Jesus in the book of Matthew:

> It hath been said, Thou shalt love thy neighbour, and hate thine enemy. But I say unto you, Love your enemies, bless them that curse you, do good to them that hate you, and pray for them which despitefully use you, and persecute you; that ye may be the children of your Father which is in heaven [Matthew 5:43–45].

CHAPTER 3

THE KAISER AND
ROBERT CAMPBELL
THE HONOR OF AN OFFICER

I n 1914 Kaiser Wilhelm II of Germany was proud and conflicted.[1] The eldest grandson of Queen Victoria of England, he had a love-hate relationship with the British. In manners and dress, he acted the part of an English nobleman. His spoken English was nearly perfect, his accent virtually indiscernible from that of his first cousin, King George V of England.

But Wilhelm resented the British for not fully accepting him as an equal in the royal circle. The British monarchy had existed for more than a thousand years and was rich in tradition and prestige. Unified Germany had come into existence only forty years earlier when Prussian chancellor Otto von Bismarck forced thirty-nine independent duchies and principalities to unite as the nation of Deutschland, or Germany.[2] Nominal power rested with the Kaiser, but Bismarck was really the one in charge. He was responsible for the astonishing rise in industrial production and modernization that turned Germany into the world's second largest economy at the dawn of the twentieth century.

Wilhelm II was the grandson of this first emperor. He came to the throne in 1888 after his father, Frederick, died of throat cancer, three months after his coronation. Wilhelm II, twenty-nine years old at the time, was a high-strung young man who clashed with Bismarck and ultimately dismissed him. Known for his vanity, Wilhelm had a volatile temper and took great offense at any perceived slight. And yet for all his failings, there was another side to him—a compassionate side that found expression in one of the most unusual events in the complicated history of the Great War.

WILHELM LIGHTS THE FUSE

Wilhelm II was determined to help Germany find her rightful place in the world as an economic power equal or superior to Britain. To achieve the international prestige he so desperately craved, Wilhelm prodded Germany into an aggressive campaign to increase the strength and power of its naval forces. Of course, this was a direct challenge to the British, who had long held worldwide dominance of the seas. It led to an early twentieth-century arms race as the two nations built massive battleships known as dreadnoughts ("dread nothing") that left their respective military leaders itching for a chance to test their power in battle.

By early 1914, the world was a powder keg. The British were tired of Germany's military posturing, and Wilhelm and his advisers were anxious to put the British in their place. The French had the largest standing army in the world and wanted an excuse to avenge their humiliating defeat in the Franco-Prussian War of 1871, which had led to the creation of a unified Germany in the first place. The Austro-Hungarian empire was deteriorating under the rule of the

Hapsburg monarchy, which was quickly losing its grip on the many competing ethnic groups it had brought together in its glory days. Russia, ruled by Tsar Nicholas II (first cousin to both Wilhelm and George V), was ripe for revolution, its peasants laboring under grinding poverty while the nobility supped in splendid grandeur in the glittering palaces of St. Petersburg and Moscow. Into this volatile mix was added discontent of workers in all the industrialized nations. Labor unions pressed for socialism as envisioned by the German-born Karl Marx and his Communist followers in Europe and America.

Attempting to contain all these forces, nations had entered into a complex web of alliances that required them to go to war when any one of them was attacked. At the beginning of 1914, no one could have predicted the awful fury that would unfold after the murder in June of the Archduke Franz Ferdinand, heir to the Austro-Hungarian empire, by a Serbian anarchist.

The way the Great War came about is a Rubik's Cube of interlocking treaties. The young man who killed the archduke was from Serbia, and Austria demanded that Serbia surrender its sovereignty as punishment. Serbia yielded to most demands but not all, which gave Austria the excuse it was looking for to go to war with Serbia. Austria did so with confidence because treaties required Germany to come to its aid in such a war. But Russia was an ally of Serbia, and so Russia began to prepare for war. France and England were allies of Russia, so they too mobilized.

Because each country's military had been mechanized, it was thought that the first nation to strike would have a massive military advantage and could probably defeat its opponent in six weeks or less. No country wanted to be last onto the field of battle. Each great nation felt that its international standing depended on knocking out the others with an overwhelming first strike.

Germany was the most aggressive, aching for the chance to show its dominance. As war loomed, politicians in France and England tried to pull back, proposing a peace conference to deal with the crisis. But the military leaders in Germany would have none of it. Even though Wilhelm himself had second thoughts, he was quickly overruled. Having stoked the fires of German nationalism for so long, he had lost control of the situation. That is how the world blew up in just a matter of weeks.

Germany almost pulled off a six weeks' war when it quickly invaded both France and Russia. The war on the Eastern Front was prosecuted successfully, but the Allies' resistance stiffened just outside Paris, and Germany could press no further. The war there settled into a macabre stalemate on the Western Front (the border between France and Germany), as troops on both sides hunkered down. The area between the opposing trenches was nothing more than a killing field. Artillery strikes launched hundreds of thousands of tons of explosives and poisonous gas against the enemy. Futile infantry charges into rapid-fire machine guns that killed thousands of men at a time became the norm. These new battlefield conditions stymied generals on both sides, and millions died while each side tried to gain the advantage.

By 1918, when the war finally ended, 16 million people had been killed and 20 million wounded. Wilhelm II was forced to abdicate, and he lived out his life in exile in the Netherlands. The Bolsheviks, led by Lenin, had withdrawn from the Great War altogether to create a new nightmare at home. The ragged ending of the war forced Germany to surrender unconditionally, even though German forces had not been beaten on the field of battle. The Armistice ending hostilities on the Western Front and the subsequent Treaty of Versailles set the stage for World War II. War reparations hobbled Germany's economy, which contributed to the worldwide Great Depression. And much of the responsibility for World War I fell on the shoulders of the vain little man who ruled

Germany, all for the lack of a little respect from the British. Of course, it's more complicated than that, but Wilhelm's vanity did contribute mightily to the tragedy.

BRITISH ARMY CAPTAIN ROBERT CAMPBELL

Captain Robert Campbell was a professional soldier from Gravesend, Kent, in southeastern England, who joined the British army in 1903. When World War I broke out in August 1914, twenty-nine-year-old Captain Campbell was assigned command of the First Battalion of the East Surrey Regiment. His battalion was transported to France, where it took up position on the Monds-Conde canal to await the expected arrival of German forces. The action started just a week later.

Captain Campbell was injured in a short battle and taken prisoner. The Germans transferred him to a hospital in Cologne on the Rhine River in northern Germany. After a period of recovery, he was taken by train to a Central Powers' prisoner of war camp in Magdeburg on the Elbe River in Saxony, far into the interior of Germany. There he languished for the next two years.

Then, in 1916, he received a letter from home telling him that his mother, Louise, was dying of cancer. At the suggestion of the commandant of the prison camp, who offered to send the letter up the chain of command with the recommendation that the leave be granted, the heartbroken Campbell wrote to Kaiser Wilhelm II asking permission to return home to see his mother one last time before her death. He promised to return to Magdeburg after this requested leave.

To the astonishment not just of Campbell but of officials in Germany, America, and England as well, the Kaiser granted his request for "compassionate leave." His parole allowed him to leave the prison camp for two weeks' leave. The only requirement the Kaiser placed on Campbell was that he promise to return on his "honour as a British Army officer." He gave his word, and telegraphs started chattering to make it happen.[3]

Because Great Britain and Germany had broken off diplomatic relations at the beginning of the war, it was impossible for the two parties to communicate directly with each other. In 1916, the United States was not a combatant and was therefore chosen as an intermediary to broker the deal. The correspondence that developed is fascinating. A letter from the United States embassy in London gives us an idea of the complicated arrangements that had to be made:

> American Embassy, London. No. 1193.
>
> The American Ambassador presents his compliments to His Majesty's Secretary of State for Foreign Affairs, and has the honour to transmit herewith enclosed a copy of a letter he has received from the Charge d'Affairs at Berlin, dated the 6th instant, referring to the telegram communicated to Viscount Grey on the 6th of November and enclosing a copy of Note Verbale from the German Government concerning the permission granted to Captain R. C. Campbell to go to England for 14 days.[4]

Getting Campbell home required very complex logistics: transfer him by train to a neutral country; hand him over to the authorities there; allow him to travel unescorted to England, where he was duty bound to report to his army superiors; and then go by train to his mother's home in Gravesend. At the end of his visit, he needed to do the process in reverse. Of course, all of that required travel documents, copies of his parole from the Kaiser, and the cooperation of multiple countries and jurisdictions. Plus, once in England, the British army could easily keep him there. In fact, it was crazy to expect that they would allow him to return to prison. And yet somehow all the parties completed the arrangements.

Another memo, dated November 6, 1916, shows that Campbell first went to neutral Holland in the Netherlands, where he was given transport across the English Channel. The memo confirmed that he arrived at Gravesend on November 7 and was granted a "fortnight's leave of absence on parole from internment at Magdeburg Germany."[5]

Remarkably, everything came together for Captain Campbell, who spent a full week with his mother before keeping his promise to return to Germany. His mother passed away three months later.

British historian Richard van Emden characterized this generosity by the Kaiser as an act of chivalry that was extremely rare, even in World War I. "Captain Campbell was an officer, and he made a promise on his honour to go back," said van Emden. "Had he not turned up there would not have been any retribution on any other prisoners. What I think is more amazing is that the British army let him go back to Germany. The British could have said to him, 'You're not going back. You're going to stay here.'"[6]

But the British army did allow him to go back. Although British authorities allowed no other such exchanges during the war, they permitted Campbell to keep his word. With his return to Magdeburg prison camp, he had fulfilled his duty to the Kaiser.

Now he went to work to fulfill his duty to England. For the next nine months, Campbell and other prisoners surreptitiously dug an escape tunnel. They succeeded in getting out of the prisoner of war camp and somehow managed to travel from eastern Germany to the border of the Netherlands. They were recaptured before they could cross the border, however, and were returned to Magdeburg for the duration of the war.

Campbell was sent back to England after the war ended in 1918 and served in the British military until 1925. In 1939, at the outbreak of World War II, he rejoined the military as the chief observer of the Royal Observer Corps on the Isle of Wight, in the English Channel. He served there for the duration of the war. Campbell died on the Isle of Wight in July 1966 at the age of eighty-one, his story unique in the annals of World War I.

A COMPLICATED MAN

Kaiser Wilhelm II was a complicated man whose words and actions contributed to a war that wrecked great empires and left Europe in shambles. Yet in the midst of all of that turmoil, he responded with humanity to an earnest plea from a captured British officer to visit his dying mother. Unfortunately, the written record leaves no traces of how the Kaiser felt about this. But the simple fact that he granted the request shows a poignant side of a man who is otherwise judged harshly by history.

CHAPTER 4

EDITH CAVELL
THE ULTIMATE SACRIFICE

On March 17, 1920, Dowager Queen Alexandra dedicated a marble statue to the memory of Edith Cavell, a British nurse who managed a hospital in occupied Belgium in the early years of World War I.[1] The statue, located in the heart of London at St. Martin's Place, just outside the northeast corner of Trafalgar Square, is a tribute to a woman who captured the hearts of freedom-loving people all over the Western world when she died at the hands of a German firing squad on October 12, 1915.

Edith's crime was helping more than a thousand Allied soldiers trapped behind enemy lines to find refuge in her hospital and then escape to Holland. This secret activity took place over the course of more than a year, under the nose of the increasingly suspicious German army of occupation. It went on even as Cavell and her nurses gave medical care to many hundreds of German, Belgian, English, and French patients, both military and civilian. And they did all this in one of the first modern hospitals in the world.

Edith Cavell shouldered immense pressure to carry on her secret activities as well as her public work, all while avoiding suspicion. But she was committed to rendering aid, in whatever form was required. She bore these burdens with dignity and poise right up through her capture and execution.

Viewed as a patriot by England and the United States, Cavell saw herself more simply. She just wanted to help those who suffered or who were in danger of capture. She and her nurses assisted Allied soldiers to escape even as they cared for wounded German soldiers.

It is certain that when Edith went to Brussels she had no idea that fate would issue such a challenge. It really came down to just one moment, when a member of the Belgian resistance showed up at her door with two escaped British soldiers. It would have been prudent to turn them away. But mercy dictated otherwise.

DAUGHTER OF AN ANGLICAN PRIEST

Born into a middle-class family, Edith Cavell grew up in Swardeston, a small village near Norwich in the county of Norfolk on England's east coast. Her father, the Reverend Frederick Cavell, was vicar of the Anglican church in Swardeston for nearly fifty years. As such, he had a prominent role in community life. He was a highly educated man, who made certain that his four children were diligent in their studies. Young Edith learned math, literature, and philosophy under his guidance until, at age sixteen, she went away to boarding schools.

She was a confident young woman with both athletic and artistic ability. She loved to dance. One Christmas season she danced so often that her feet bled, ruining her new shoes.[2] She looked at the world through intelligent eyes and captured its beauty in watercolors. Her skill as an illustrator could easily have developed into a career, as the figures of children came to life under her hand. But it was to the new profession of nursing that she was drawn. It became a passion that set the course of her future.

Having settled on her goal, Edith began training as a nurse at the London Hospital in 1896. She was a diligent student who followed in the footsteps of the first professional nurse, Florence Nightingale, in her standards of sanitation and professionalism.

FLORENCE NIGHTINGALE

The daughter of wealthy and God-fearing parents, Florence Nightingale felt called to render service to God by becoming a nurse. Her mother fiercely resisted her daughter's wish because she felt it was below her station.

But Florence was determined, and she pursued her vocation with zeal. She gained international notice as the leader of a contingent of nurses who served the British army in Istanbul during the Crimean War. Although the role of germs in causing disease was not yet known, she insisted that good hygiene and healthy living conditions improved a wounded soldier's chance of survival.

This philosophy contrasted starkly with abysmal conditions in most hospitals at the time, particularly military field hospitals. Dirty water, dirty clothes, dank air, and fetid ventilation all interfered with the recovery of wounded soldiers. Nurses and doctors seldom washed their hands, even after treating diseased bodies or performing surgery. They moved from one patient to the next, spreading infection and germs indiscriminately. And few hospitals opened windows or doors to let in light and fresh air. Few doctors and nurses lived past middle age, often dying from the diseases they treated. It is little wonder she had opposed her daughter entering this profession.

But Florence set out to change those conditions. She believed nursing should be a profession and that a nurse should be a model of clean living, excellent personal hygiene, and attention to detail. Nightingale-trained nurses wore crisp, clean uniforms. They studied medicine so they could assist doctors in surgery and patient care. They washed their hands frequently, changed dirty bedding, and provided their patients with clean clothing. Nightingale was a stickler for providing fresh air and lots of sunshine.

One of the ways she instituted change was to begin a campaign of public prodding by writing letters to newspapers in England. Her purpose was to goad the British government into improving hospital conditions for the troops. Eventually, this pressure caused the government to engage Isambard Kingdom Brunel to design a prefabricated field hospital to be shipped to the front lines.[3] Nightingale then had the physical facilities in which to offer much-improved patient care. The strict hygiene observed by the nursing staff reduced the death rate of injured soldiers by more than 90 percent when compared to other military hospitals. The reports from soldiers served by Nightingale and her staff made her a hero back in England.

At the conclusion of the Crimean War, she returned to London, where she used her fame to professionalize the field of nursing by establishing protocols to certify nurses. In 1860 she established a permanent nursing school at St. Thomas Hospital.

Before that time, nursing in civilian hospitals was just as bad as it was in military hospitals, with nurses working as little more than chambermaids in dirty clothes while serving in wretched conditions. Beginning with Nightingale, nurses wore clean uniforms, washed their hands frequently, rendered medical assistance to doctors, and administered medications. The effects of her training were revolutionary in increasing the chances of patients' recovering.

Another of Nightingale's great contributions to nursing was her extensive writing. She became skilled at writing training manuals for nurses that were used in other training institutions throughout the

British Empire and in the United States. Her lessons were still in use when Edith Cavell entered the profession nearly forty years after the Crimean War ended.

Nightingale also wrote tracts on hygiene and cleanliness that could be understood by nearly everyone in British society, including those who were barely literate. In this way she changed British home life for the better. When she died in 1910, she was famous around the world for her many contributions to the profession of nursing.

LEADERSHIP OF A NURSES' SCHOOL

Although there is no record of Edith Cavell ever meeting Florence Nightingale, they clearly were cut from the same cloth. Each could have led a comfortable and easy life without the risks, drudgery, and exposure required of nurses. Both Nightingale and Cavell were courted by prominent men but instead of marrying chose to devote their full energies to teaching and practicing nursing.

In 1907 Edith accepted the position of matron of the Berkendael Institute in Brussels, Belgium. She was invited there by Dr. Antoine Depage, a fierce critic of the primitive state of nursing in Belgium. Depage insisted that Belgium needed a professional school to train nurses and that its first matron be English, fluent in French, and trained at a great English nursing school. Edith Cavell met all those requirements.[4]

Thus it was that Edith left her home in England to live in the capital of a foreign country. Under her industrious direction, the school became an immediate success. Students came from Belgium, France, the Netherlands, and Germany. Cavell and Dr. Depage formed a powerful partnership that became an inspiration to the entire European continent.

SMALL ACTS IN THE GREAT WAR

There were many misconceptions at the outbreak of the Great War. For example, both sides—the Allies (Britain and France) on the one hand and the Central Powers (Germany and the Austro-Hungarian empire) on the other—thought the war would be over in a few weeks.

Virtually no one envisioned a world war of four years' duration. Nor could anyone have predicted the horror of more than 36 million military and civilian casualties, including 16 million dead and 20 million wounded.[5] In such a maelstrom of destruction, Edith Cavell's contribution might have gone unnoticed, but hundreds of Allied soldiers' lives were saved by her direct intervention, in addition to the hundreds who received medical care in her hospital.

Heroic deeds often inspire others far beyond their immediate setting and moment in time. So it was with Edith Cavell. When her arrest and execution were reported in Britain, Canada, the United States, and elsewhere, the effect was electrifying. Thousands of volunteers in all these countries, and even countries as far away as Australia and New Zealand, signed up to fight. Her execution galvanized public opinion in the United States in favor of entering the war on the side of the Allies. Many young women were inspired by her example to become nurses. And Germany was shamed into sparing the lives of the prisoners arrested with Edith.

Edith Cavell's life became an example that resonates through time. Today, the nurses' training school in Brussels is named the École Edith Cavell. A statue of her is displayed in the gardens of the Tuileries at the Louvre Museum in Paris. And in Canada Mt. Cavell bears her name, as does the Cavell Glacier in the Rocky Mountains in the United States.[6]

A MOMENT OF MERCY THAT
CHANGED EVERYTHING

The first decision Edith had to make at the outbreak of war in the summer of 1914 was whether to stay in Belgium or return to England. Of course her family and friends urged her to return home. But she firmly declared that she was needed at the school to continue teaching. She knew there would be many injured soldiers requiring care. So, that was that.

The second decision, whether to join the underground network to help Allied soldiers to safety, was thrust on her quite unexpectedly. It happened in mid-October 1914 when a member of the Belgian resistance appeared at Edith's door with two escaped British prisoners of war who had come under his care.

Herman Capiau was an engineer from Mons who had decided to resist the Germans by helping British, French, and Belgian soldiers escape from occupied Belgium. In the turmoil of war, it was relatively common for Allied soldiers at the front to find themselves suddenly surrounded by the enemy with no way back to their own lines. Sometimes they were taken prisoner. Other times they hid until the enemy troops moved on. Then they would try to find their way back to safety. If the battlefront had shifted, however, they often were unable to do so. Then they hoped to encounter sympathetic civilians who would help them find food, shelter, and safe passage to Holland. From there they could make their way to safety in England. In time, the network of people willing to help grew into a formal organization of which Capiau was a part.

On the night in question, Capiau had helped Colonel Dudley Boger and Sergeant Fred Meachin find their way from the south of Belgium to Brussels on the north coast. Boger and Meachin had been wounded on the battlefield and taken prisoner by the German army. After several weeks of recuperating in a lightly guarded hospital, they escaped and were aided by the Belgian support network.

Now, Capiau had taken them by train to the Belgian capital. Capiau tried to find shelter for them in the homes of several sympathizers, but the risk was judged too great. Almost as an afterthought, Dr. Depage's wife, who had also turned them away, suggested they might try Edith Cavell. She had an extensive campus of buildings to hide in and many beds available. So it was that the three men showed up on Edith's doorstep.

Colonel Boger's foot was badly infected, caused by poor treatment at the German hospital, followed by weeks of hiding. When asked if she could help them until he healed, Edith Cavell weighed the options. To take them in was to place her own life at risk and would require the cooperation of all her nurses, whose own lives would thereby also be at risk. Because her hospital now operated under the auspices of the International Red Cross, the potential repercussions of using a Red Cross hospital to facilitate escaping prisoners of war were ominous.

Even so, after hearing their story, Cavell agreed to take them in. Later, she used her own money to hire a guide to help the soldiers make their way to the Netherlands, a neutral country. She knew that if they made it to that point, they could get safely to England. That is why she became the focus of German suspicion—helping soldiers escape to fight another day was clearly not in the best interest of the occupying army.

Thus began Edith's involvement with the Belgian resistance. One refugee, Sergeant Jesse Tunmore, escaped from a German field hospital and spent three weeks surviving as best he could before being taken in by Auguste Joly, a member of the network. When he arrived at Edith's hospital on December 23, 1914, she welcomed him as a fellow citizen of Norwich. After a brief introduction, she moved him to the basement to hide with two other British soldiers.

Because it took time to arrange for guides and move men out without arousing suspicion, Tunmore and his companions hid there for several weeks. Edith took his photo for a fake passport, which Tunmore was to use in crossing into Holland. After a false start, caused by an error in his new passport, Edith accompanied him partway to the border between Belgium and neutral Holland. Once in the Netherlands, he learned about a pending zeppelin attack on London. He rushed back to England and passed on the information to British military authorities, who prepared extraordinary defenses to protect London from the attack. These efforts were successful, and the huge airships were unable to penetrate London's defenses. In one of the ironies of war, the ships dropped their bombs, originally intended for London, on Norfolk, the home county of Edith and Tunmore.[7]

A month after the escape of Sergeant Tunmore, and after helping ten French soldiers find their way back to Allied lines, Edith received Charlie Scott, who had spent ten months in hiding. Seriously wounded in the chest early in the war, he was in very bad shape by the time he arrived at the clinic. Edith immediately put him to bed and used her modern techniques to dress his wounds. In time he started to recover, and he and Edith shared stories of England.

Just as things seemed to be improving for Charlie Scott, he was awakened one evening by Edith, who told him in an urgent voice that she needed his help. German police had come to the clinic to search for escaped soldiers. While members of her staff diverted their attention, Edith moved Scott to an outbuilding filled with large barrels of apples. She helped him into one of the barrels and covered him with green apples. Left alone, he waited in anxious silence as the Germans made their way into the building and searched it. Fortunately, they did not check the barrel he was hiding in, and both he and Edith were spared. The next day she hired a guide to lead him to the border between Belgium and neutral Holland. By April 1915 he was safely home in England.[8]

The story of Ernest Stanton is a poignant one. Stanton, a member of the 4th Battalion, Middlesex Regiment, was left behind after the battle of Mons. He spent seven months in hiding, sheltered by a Belgian family. The stress was overwhelming for Stanton, particularly because he had to squeeze his large body into a very small water cistern under the floor when Germans came to search his protector's home. The cistern was barely large enough to conceal him, which caused much anxiety each time a search happened. By the time he reached Edith's hospital, he was so paralyzed by fear that he had lost the ability to speak.

Edith spent extra time with Stanton, talking to him late into the evenings to help draw him out of his shell. In time, the power of speech returned, and he was able to make his way back to freedom. Once home, he continued to recover. The only other time he lost his ability to speak was the day of Edith's funeral.[9]

All of this mercy, shared so freely by this strong and compassionate woman, came at a price. Edith was under constant surveillance. The stress continued to build, especially after one of the members of her network learned that a special unit had been organized to root them out. The particular focus of the two German officers in charge of this unit was to see Edith arrested and executed. Though they had no proof, they had their suspicions. It was only a matter of time.

THE END OF THE NETWORK

The first arrest of members of Edith's group came on July 31, 1915, at 10:30 P.M. Sergeant Henri Pinkhoff and six officers of the German police showed up at the home of Philippe Baucq and arrested him and Louise Thuliez, who happened to be at his home arranging for a group of Belgians to escape to Holland. Over the next five days, the Germans arrested an additional thirty-five members from towns and villages all over Belgium. Edith was warned to escape, but she chose to wait.

On the afternoon of August 5, Pinkhoff and his officers arrived at the hospital, where he proceeded to tear the place apart looking for incriminating evidence. He verbally assaulted Edith and her nursing staff before finally arresting her.[10]

Edith could have dissembled about her role in the multitude of escapes, but that violated her sense of honesty. Instead, she answered every question precisely and without elaboration. When asked if she had helped British soldiers escape, she replied that she had. Far more serious was the question whether she knew that "conducting soldiers to the enemy" was an offense punishable by death. Edith replied that she did know it, but from her point of view she had simply helped young men make their way to Holland. What they did after that was their concern, not hers.

Of course, her answer did not help her cause. On September 9, 1915, the military court found her guilty and sentenced her to death by firing squad.

Powerful individuals, including members of the American legation in Brussels and the Spanish minister to Belgium, went to work immediately to get her sentence commuted. Their attempts were in vain.

The day before her execution, Edith was visited by an Anglican chaplain, the Reverend H. Stirling Gahan. She told him, "I want my friends to know that I willingly give my life for my country. I have no fear nor shirking. I have seen death so often that it is not strange or fearful to me."

He wrote later that she also said, "Patriotism is not enough. I must have no hatred or bitterness for anyone."[11]

As their interview came to an end, the Reverend Gahan said to her, "We shall always remember you as a heroine and a martyr."

Edith replied quickly, "Don't think of me like that. Think of me only as a nurse who tried to do her duty."[12]

A steady example of courage, she remained honest and kind to the very end, even finding the strength to forgive her enemies. A German firing squad executed Edith Cavell on October 12, 1915.

"A NURSE WHO TRIED TO DO HER DUTY"

Despite her modest wish, Edith Cavell has gone down in history for far more than the nursing care she gave. The storm of protest at her execution was fierce and immediate. Public demonstrations against the Central Powers' inhumanity were held in cities around the world. So strong and so unexpected was the response that the German high command suspended the executions of others in Edith's group. The Kaiser declared that in future, Germany would not execute a woman without his personal authority. The implication was that he would not grant it.

What the Germans had not considered was the effect on public opinion of executing a respected nurse who had unselfishly rendered aid to wounded soldiers from all the warring nations. Just a few months before, the ocean liner *HMS Lusitania* had been sunk by a German submarine, ending over a thousand civilian lives, including those of more than a hundred Americans. The horror Americans felt at that brutality and disregard for common decency was reinforced by the execution of nurse Edith Cavell. The Germans' miscalculation about the effect of their actions on public opinion became a factor in the United States entering the war.

EDITH CAVELL'S LEGACY

Today, people remember Edith Cavell as an English patriot whose mercy extended to all people in need, regardless of nationality or background. She is honored for her courage in helping stranded Allied soldiers escape from Belgium. Anglican congregations throughout the world venerate her every year on October 12, the anniversary of her death.

Edith's contributions to professionalizing the new field of nursing are likewise inspiring. Her greatest legacy, however, was in showing mercy to those in need, even though mercy was not shown to her.

CHAPTER 5

OSWALD BÖELCKE
GERMAN FLYING ACE

dvances in military technology between the Revolutionary War and the Civil War were incredible, but they paled in comparison to the amazing new technology employed in World War I. Motorized vehicles made transporting troops and supplies to the battlefield much faster. Telephone lines gave instant communication between the front lines and the generals at their headquarters. Hot-air balloons and airplanes enabled observers to fly far behind enemy lines to observe precise troop positions in order to inform infantry placements. On both sides, chemical weapons injured or destroyed the lungs of thousands of soldiers, leaving them to choke in excruciating pain until death relieved them of their suffering.

The armies of both the Allied Powers and the Central Powers dug trenches that extended from the English Channel in the north to Switzerland in the south. Miserably wet and muddy, soldiers on the Western Front huddled through winters and sweltered in summers. Their generals repeatedly ordered futile attempts to break through the no-man's land between the opposing trenches. So devastating was this warfare that the British army suffered some 50,000 fatalities in a single day, more than the United States lost in the nearly ten years of the war in Vietnam.

By the end of the Great War, aviation science had leaped forward as the demands of aerial combat called for continual improvements in airplane design and power. In many respects, World War I brought about the age of air travel that we now take for granted.

During the immediate aftermath of the war, some writers portrayed aerial combatants as knights of the air engaged in a modern form of chivalrous combat. The truth was harsher than that. America's first and best ace, Captain Edward (Eddie) V. Rickenbacker, said, "Fighting in the air is not a sport. It is scientific murder."[1] Aerial combat pitted one man against another in a life-and-death struggle that meant death or imprisonment for one or the other or both. It was kill or be killed.

One pilot well known for his successful engagements in the air was Oswald Böelcke, the first German flying ace. By the time he died in battle, he had shot down at least forty Allied aircraft, almost double the number of Rickenbacker's. Böelcke's record was exceeded only by that of Captain Manfred von Richthofen, the Red Baron, who was also from Germany and is credited with at least eighty victories in aerial combat. But Böelcke was the master. Throughout his life, Richthofen ascribed his success to Böelcke's superb leadership and mentoring.

Fortunately for history, both Böelcke and Richthofen left written records. Böelcke wrote *An Aviator's Field Book,* and Richthofen, *The Red Battle Flyer.* In America, Rickenbacker wrote *Fighting the Flying Circus,* describing how an American unit gained success against the German squadron led by Richthofen. From these first-hand accounts, we gain insight into the remarkable young men who were thrust into a new type of battle at the violent beginning of the twentieth century. Yet in spite of the incredible demands he faced as a fighter pilot, as well as the renown he achieved, Colonel Oswald Böelcke retained his compassion and personal decency. A number of stories demonstrate those qualities, but one stands out because of his willingness to fulfill a potentially deadly request.

BÖELCKE DELIVERS A LETTER

Air battles were fought at close quarters. To be successful, a pilot had to draw close enough to his opponent that his shots would hit the enemy aircraft. Böelcke did what was required to win the battle for his country, but he felt no personal animosity against the enemy pilots he engaged. Manfred von Richthofen wrote of Böelcke:

> It is strange that everybody who met Böelcke imagined that he alone was his true friend. I have made the acquaintance of about forty men, each of whom imagined that he alone was Böelcke's intimate. Each imagined that he had the monopoly of Böelcke's affections. Men whose names were unknown to Böelcke believed that he was particularly fond of them. This is a curious phenomenon which I have never noticed in anyone else. Böelcke had not a personal enemy. He was equally polite to everybody, making no differences.[2]

Böelcke also made unlikely friends of two Englishmen whose airplane caught fire because of his actions. A contemporary wrote about the choice pilots in burning airplanes had to make: "On two or three occasions pilots have gallantly stuck to their controls and have managed to land safely in blazing machines from fully 1,000 feet. There is a general opinion that it is possible to fit a parachute so that in the event of an aeroplane catching fire, the pilot and passenger can quit it at once and descend safely."[3]

Nothing was done to test this theory, however. Pilots whose aircraft were disabled had the terrible choice of riding the aircraft to the ground or jumping to their death. It was a particularly horrifying choice when the aircraft was on fire.

The two English fliers whose airplane Böelcke disabled in January 1916 were able to land. He wrote of the incident:

> On the 5th of January, I pursued two Englishmen, overtook them and attacked the first one. The other did not seem to see me; at any rate he kept right on. The fight was comparatively short. I attacked, he defended himself; I hit and he didn't. He had dropped considerably in the meantime and finally started to sway and landed. I stayed close behind him so he could not escape. Close to headquarters he landed; his machine broke apart, the pilot jumped out and collapsed. I quickly landed and found the 'plane already surrounded by people from the nearby village.[4]

The two English officers were Lieutenant William Somervill (pilot) and Lieutenant Geoffrey Formilli (observer). In one account of the incident, Böelcke said, "I went straight up to the Englishmen, shook hands with them and told them I was delighted to have brought them down alive."[5]

Formilli tested Böelcke's sincerity later by asking him if he could get a letter into English hands that Formilli had written to his captain, telling him that both Somervill and he were alive but had been shot down by one of Germany's most famous pilots.

Böelcke assured him he would try, and try he did. He flew behind British lines while dodging enemy ground fire to reach the base of the pilots he had taken down. There he dropped the letter. The British, after reviewing it, sent it on to Formilli's mother.[6]

BÖELCKE TAKES AN ENEMY
FLYER OUT FOR COFFEE

As the number of Böelcke's successful air strikes climbed, he became a hero in Germany. His forty combat victories gave the German people something to cheer about, even though they were insignificant compared to the battles in the trenches, where deaths were measured in the millions. People could easily grasp the numbers in the air warfare and root for individual successes.

To celebrate his accomplishments, Böelcke was taken from the battlefront against his wishes and sent on a tour of several cities and military centers in Central Powers countries. After he returned to active service, he had an amiable encounter with an Englishman on the ground after a rough encounter with him in the air:

> One of them thought he could get me . . . and followed me. A little apart from the rest, I offered battle, and soon I had him. I did not let him go; he had no more ammunition left. In descending, he swayed heavily from side to side. As he said later, this was involuntary; I had crippled his machine. He came down northeast of [location undisclosed]. The aviator jumped out of his burning machine and beat about with hands and feet, for he was also on fire. I went home to get fresh supplies of cartridges and start anew, for more Englishmen were coming. But I had no success.
>
> Yesterday I got the Englishman, whom I had captured, from the prisoners' camp and took him to the Casino for coffee. I showed him our aviation field and learned a lot of interesting things from him.[7]

BÖELCKE TAKEN DOWN

On October 28, 1916, Böelcke engaged in air combat alongside two of his closest comrades, Manfred von Richthofen and Erwin

Boehm. Having lost track of each other during the battle, Boehm and Böelcke closed in on the same enemy aircraft. Into their close quarters came Richthofen in a dive against another enemy aircraft. When Böelcke swerved to miss Richthofen, his upper wing collided with Boehm's landing gear, tearing the fabric from Böelcke's wing and rendering it useless. Böelcke started an immediate descent. Though his aircraft did make a relatively soft landing, Böelcke had neglected to cinch his restraining belts. He was thrown forward into the instrument panel and killed.

Boehm was so devastated by the news that he had unintentionally caused Böelcke's death that he had to be talked out of committing suicide. He later wrote a marvelous tribute to Oswald Böelcke:

> Now everything is so empty to us. Only little by little does it come fully to our consciousness, that within the gap which our Böelcke leaves, the soul of the total is missing. He was nevertheless in each relationship our leader and master. He had an irresistible influence on all, even on superiors, which had to do purely with his personality, and the all-naturalness of his being. He could take us everywhere. We never had the feeling that anything could fail if he were there, and almost everything succeeded as well. In this one and a half months he has been with us, we have put over 60 hostile aeroplanes out of action and made the dominance of the Englishmen shrink from day to day. Now we all must see that his triumphant spirit does not sink.

Oswald Böelcke was a remarkable man who had been called into the service of his country at a young age. He was only twenty-five when he died, but he left a lasting imprint on the men he led and the men he fought, as well as an indelible imprint in aviation history. He was a war hero who extended grace to his defeated enemy when a battle was over.

TRIBUTES TO THE EARLY PILOTS

President Theodore Roosevelt said of the fighter pilots of the Great War, "An ordinary air fighter is an extraordinary man and the extraordinary air fighter stands as one in a million among his fellows."[8] Living in constant danger of annihilation, these men fought on as required by their country.

Modern fighter pilot Jerry R. Caddick provided a searing description of air combat:

> Fighter pilots, above all else, know who among their peers are hunters and who are hunted. They absolutely will not fly into a tough combat situation with a wingman they don't trust and not all men make the cut. Where we work is a vicious place. I'll attempt to describe it, but the full comprehension comes only in a sky full of hot metal and smart missiles that all seem to be looking at you. You're in a machine that is so fast and powerful that you intuitively know that if death comes, it will be full of hot fire. Frail human that you are, you will be shredded to pieces. Worst of all, you'll be alone in a fierce place where your comrades cannot hold you while you die. That is the real environment of a fighter pilot.[9]

Winston Churchill said of the fighter pilots of the Royal Air Force in World War II, "Never in the field of human conflict was so much owed by so many to so few."[10]

That men such as Oswald Böelcke could maintain their humanity in the face of war is a tribute to human goodness.

CHAPTER 6

EDITH WHARTON

A SEASON OF MERCY

Edith Wharton, a world-renowned novelist of the early twentieth century, was the first woman to win the Pulitzer Prize, which was awarded for her highly acclaimed novel, *The Age of Innocence*. She received three nominations for the Nobel Prize in literature as well. During the Great War, she was a front-line journalist on the battlefields in France.

Having been born into the highest levels of New York society in 1865, Edith Wharton documented the strict rules and formality that governed the lives of New York's most notable citizens. She was well equipped to do that. Born Edith Newbold Jones, she was part of the family about whom the phrase "keeping up with the Joneses" originated.[1]

Edith's prose is scintillating and elegant, filled with clever insights and sometimes biting social commentary. Writing as an insider, she brought the closed world of New York's elite society to vibrant life as she described attending operas and grand balls, riding in elegant brougham carriages, dining in exclusive parties in gilded townhouses, and spending summers socializing in extravagant luxury in the mansions of Newport, Rhode Island. Her accounts of everyday life in a rarefied social stratum have fascinated millions of readers for more than a hundred years. Some of her books became the basis for popular movies.

With both fame and fortune to support a comfortably elegant lifestyle, Edith Wharton might easily have been dismissed as a talented dilettante. But doing so would overlook the remarkable contributions she made during World War I to relieve the suffering of refugees and those stricken with tuberculosis. She was born into luxury and comfort but risked her life on the front lines of battle to aid those displaced by war and disease.

THE AGE OF INNOCENCE

That I was born into a world in which telephones, motors, electric light, central heating . . . , X-rays, cinemas, radium, aero planes and wireless telegraphy were not only unknown but still mostly unforeseen, may seem the most striking difference between then and now; but the really vital change is that, in my youth, the Americans of the original States, who in moments of crisis still shaped the national point of view, were the heirs of an old tradition of European culture which the country has now totally rejected. This rejection (which Mr. Walter Lippmann regards as the chief cause of the country's present moral impoverishment) has opened a gulf between those days and these. The compact world of my youth has receded into a past from which it can only be dug up in bits by the assiduous relic-hunter;

and its smallest fragments begin to be worth collecting
and putting together before the last of those who knew
the live structure are swept away with it.[2]

It is impossible today to fully imagine the world as it is existed before the Great War. Dozens of monarchies were swept away by the war
to be replaced by repressive dictatorships in Russia, Germany, Spain,
and elsewhere. Even the great republics, including the United States
and Britain, appeared doomed when the Great Depression settled in.
The fragile balance of international economic systems interacting with
one another came crashing down in a combination of events precipi-
tated by the war. Edith Wharton was a witness to all of that.

But to Wharton and others of her class, the social changes that
followed the war were equally devastating as society rejected the
leadership of a social elite that had been built up over nearly three
hundred years of American history. She was never sentimental about
rigid rules that kept people in their place, but she did recognize that
with their passing something of great value was lost:

> My readers, by this time, may be wondering what
> were the particular merits, private or civic, of these
> amiable persons. Their lives, as one looks back, cer-
> tainly seem lacking in relief; but I believe their value
> lay in upholding two standards of importance in any
> community, that of education and good manners, and
> of scrupulous probity in business and private affairs.
> New York has always been a commercial community,
> and in my infancy the merits and defects of its citizens
> were those of a mercantile middle class. The first duty
> of such a class was to maintain a strict standard of up-
> rightness in affairs; and the gentlemen of my father's
> day did maintain it, whether in the law, in banking,
> shipping or wholesale commercial enterprises. I well
> remember the horror excited by any irregularity in

affairs, and the relentless social ostracism inflicted on the families of those who lapsed from professional or business integrity. In one case, where two or three men of high social standing were involved in a discreditable bank failure, their families were made to suffer to a degree that would seem merciless to our modern judgment. But perhaps the New Yorkers of that day were unconsciously trying to atone for their culpable neglect of state and national politics, from which they had long disdainfully held aloof, by upholding the sternest principles of business probity, and inflicting the severest social penalties on whoever lapsed from them. At any rate I should say that the qualities justifying the existence of our old society were social amenity and financial incorruptibility; and we have travelled far enough from both to begin to estimate their value.[3]

In this excerpt from Wharton's autobiography can be discerned both her remarkable grace in writing and the values she felt were lacking in the postwar world. For lovers of history, reading her books is a wonderful way to step back in time to a world that no longer exists.

PROVIDING RELIEF TO THE SUFFERING

Edith spent several years as a child living abroad with her family in Italy, France, and England. After her marriage to Edward Wharton at age twenty-three, she and her husband took exotic cruises and spent years living in the great cities of Europe. Then Edward's health began to fail. They found that spending their winters in Paris, instead of Boston, provided him some relief. Ultimately, as Edith's writing career flourished, the Whartons decided to spend most of their time in France. Unfortunately, Edward's mental health failed along with his physical health. He fought deep bouts of depression, which was judged to be incurable. In 1913 Edith divorced her husband and moved to France permanently.[4]

At the outbreak of war in August 1914, Edith found herself without access to any money as France mobilized for war. It was not that she had no money—a trust fund provided her a generous allowance, which she had in addition to royalties from her publications. Rather, the Paris banks refused to transfer currency at a time of national crisis. She had to scramble to find ways to pay her servants and her rent, falling behind on all accounts. Since everyone at the time believed that the war between Germany and the Allied Powers would last no more than six weeks, most of her friends advised her to go to England for the duration.[5]

But Wharton decided to stay in her adopted country, particularly when the Comtesse d'Haussonville asked her to assist the Red Cross in creating employment for local French women. With so many men suddenly drafted into the army, most Paris hotels, restaurants, and work-houses were closed.

Wharton recorded that though she had no experience in either organizing relief efforts or supervising a work-room, she did discover a knack for finding resources. When the women in her district came together to discuss what they could do to aid the war effort, it was discovered that they had some highly skilled seamstresses in the group. They decided to start making women's lingerie. By asking her many French friends whose bank accounts were not frozen, she was able to raise 12,000 francs, a very large amount of money at the time. She found another benefactor who offered the use of a large empty apartment to set up operations.

Rather than compete with the many other such groups that were making hospital clothing in anticipation of war casualties, Wharton's group set out to make high quality, stylish lingerie that could be sold for profit both in Paris and in the United States in order to support the cause. Their business caught on quickly, and soon Edith

Wharton's contacts in France and America had set up a distribution network. In addition to women's clothing, they also started making men's shirts and other specialty items. With Wharton as a driving force, this small business flourished.[6]

When it became clear that the war would last much longer than six weeks and cause far greater destruction and suffering than ever imagined, Wharton helped form a new charity, the *Accueil Franco-Américain* ("French-American Welcoming"). Through this charity, she raised money in America to help resettle refugees displaced by the war in Belgium and border areas between Germany and France. It was a huge success.

By the signing of the Armistice, which ended the war in 1918, five thousand refugees were settled in Paris. Four facilities had also been established to care for women and children with tuberculosis. These facilities were well staffed and promoted a high standard of sanitation.

To achieve such remarkable results, she and her fellow volunteers engaged in endless fundraising. One traveled to America with letters of introduction from Wharton, with which she raised large sums of money. When their efforts required even more money, Edith Wharton used her unique talents in an unusual way. She sent invitations to famous artists and authors in Europe and America to submit original poems, drawings, and articles to be included in a small book entitled *The Book of the Homeless*. Her goal was to sell the book, with all profits going to support her charity.

Wharton contributed to the book as well as compiling and editing it, and she personally translated French and Italian submissions into English. The book became a best seller in the United States and Europe. She offered the original manuscript for sale at a charity auction in New York, which brought in even more money to support the relief effort.

Although supremely self-confident, Edith Wharton was also

modest, always praising her fellow volunteers for their contributions of both time and money:

> I cannot end this summary of our war-labours without speaking of the response from America which alone made it possible for me to go on with the work. From my cousin Lewis Ledyard and his friend Payne Whitney, whose generosity built for us the sanatorium of La Tuyolle, to the woman doctor who sold her tiny scrap of radium because she had no other means of helping, and the French and English servants in New York who again and again sent us their joint savings, we met on every side with inexhaustible encouragement and sympathy. 'Edith Wharton' committees were formed in New York, Boston, Washington, Philadelphia and Providence, and friends and strangers worked with me at a distance as untiringly as those who were close at hand. I should like to tell them all now that I have never forgotten what they did.[7]

REPORTING FROM THE FRONT LINES

> Early in 1915 the French Red Cross asked me to report on the needs of some military hospitals near the front. Common prudence should have made me refuse to beg for more money; but in those days it never occurred to any one to evade a request of that kind. Armed with the needful permits, and my car laden to the roof with bundles of hospital supplies, I set out to inspect the fever hospital at Chalons-sur-Marne. What I saw there made me feel the urgency of telling my rich and generous compatriots something of the desperate needs of the hospitals in the war zone.[8]

Wharton wrote a powerful article about her impressions of the war that appeared in *Scribner's Magazine.* It was so successful in influencing American opinion that General Joseph Joffre, commander of the French forces on the Western Front, waived the usual prohibition against journalists going to the front lines. Wharton made six dangerous visits to the front. From these visits, and in between her charitable work, she wrote a hugely successful series of articles for *Scribner's* that gained nationwide interest.

Her articles were consolidated into the book *Fighting France,* which became a best seller, providing more funds for her relief efforts. It is also one of the few historical sources that give a noncombatant's view of the war. She was particularly successful in capturing the shifting moods of life near the front lines. Consider this gem:

> To the chance observer, Verdun appears to live only in its hospitals; and of these there are fourteen within the walls alone. As darkness fell, the streets became completely deserted, and the cannonade seemed to grow nearer and more incessant. That first night the hush was so intense that every reverberation from the dark hills beyond the walls brought out in the mind its separate vision of destruction; and then, just as the strained imagination could bear no more, the thunder ceased. A moment later, in a court below my windows, a pigeon began to coo; and all night long the two sounds strangely alternated.[9]

To those who have experienced war only in books and movies, it appears that every moment is filled with fighting and calamity. But in real war, there are intense bursts of activity followed by periods of prolonged idleness. For some, the breaks provide much needed relief. For others, such breaks only increase tension because violence can erupt at any time without warning.

On one of her later visits to the front, Edith Wharton stood within a few feet of German soldiers. Both sides knew the enemy was just a few feet away, but neither side attacked because no orders had been given. Thus did human beings live under the constant torture of suspense and anxiety.

Adding to Wharton's personal anxiety was the lack of professional attention in the very facilities that aimed to save people's lives. Modern military hospitals are wonders of efficiency and sanitation—built to protect the wounded from infections and disease. Such was not the case in World War I. Wharton described conditions on one of her visits:

> In the doorway our passage was obstructed by a mountain of damp straw which a gang of hostler-soldiers were pitch-forking out of the aisles. The interior of the church was dim and suffocating. Between the pillars hung screens of plaited straw, forming little enclosures in each of which about a dozen sick men lay on more straw, without mattresses or blankets. No beds, no tables, no chairs, no washing appliances—in their muddy clothes, as they come from the front, they are bedded down on the stone floor like cattle till they are well enough to go back to their job.[10]

A MOMENT OF DECISION—A SEASON OF MERCY

For her efforts in the Great War, Edith Wharton was appointed by the president of France as a chevalier of the Legion of Honor, the nation's highest civilian award. Thus, the woman who grew up in the lap of luxury proved herself to have stern resolve and undaunted courage. Many thousands of lives were blessed by her efforts.

For Wharton, the decision that changed her life was choosing to stay in Paris at the outbreak of World War I, rather than return to safety in England or the United States. The consequence was that she endured four years of warfare while engaging in tireless acts of charity, sometimes at the peril of her life. For five long years, including the war years and a year of healing that followed, Edith

Wharton put her own interests aside to render aid to thousands of people. Her season of mercy forever changed her life and that of many others for the better.

AN OUTSIZED IMPACT

Having risked her life to give comfort to the wounded and having spent much of her fortune organizing relief efforts on a heroic scale, Edith Wharton could easily have returned to a comfortable and uncomplicated life in the United States. From a childhood and youth in the Age of Innocence, in which considerable time was spent in attending formal teas and lavish banquets, to adulthood amid the harsh realities of war, she became a woman of substance, honored by both her native and her adopted countries. She wrote:

> On the 14th of July 1919 I stood on the high balcony of a friend's house in the Champs Elysees (in Paris), and saw the Allied Armies ride under the Arch of Triumph, and down the storied avenue to the misty distance of the Place de la Concorde and its obelisk of flame. As I stood there, high over the surging crowds and the great procession, the midsummer sun blinding my eyes, and the significance of that incredible spectacle dazzling my heart, I remembered what Bergson had once said of my inability to memorize great poetry: "You're dazzled by it." Yes, I thought; I shan't remember all this except as a golden blur of emotion. Even now I can't catch the details, I can't separate the massed flags, or distinguish the famous generals as they ride by, or the names of the regiments as they pass. I remember thankfully that a grand motile for whom I have secured a wheeled chair must have received it just in time to join his group in the Place de la Concorde. . . . The rest is all a glory of shooting sunrays reflected from shining arms and helmets, from

the flanks of glossy chargers, the dark glitter of the "seventy-fives" [field artillery], of machine-guns and tanks. But all those I had seen at the front, dusty, dirty, mud-encrusted, blood-stained, spent and struggling on; when I try to remember, the two visions merge into one, and my heart is broken with them.[11]

CHAPTER 7

HERR ROSENAU AND ALEX LURYE

CAST THY BREAD UPON THE WATERS

Philosophers suggest that for an act to qualify as compassionate or humane, it should be done with no thought of compensation. A compassionate person acts in the interest of another simply because it is the right thing to do. Such acts are born out of empathy and kindness and often require sacrifice from the one who gives. Such was the case of a Jewish man in Germany who showed kindness to an American soldier in the last days of World War I. He did so, never imagining that one day his simple gesture of kindness would save his family from destruction.

AMERICA ENTERS THE WAR

The United States declared war on the Central Powers, led by Germany, on April 6, 1917. Though their troops and armor were not yet fully deployed at that point, American participation in the war was crucial to the victory of the Allied Powers. The arrival of two million American soldiers, with the promise of up to six million more, convinced ordinary German soldiers that defeat was inevitable. The Central Powers simply did not have enough young men to equal the combined strength of the Allies. Troop morale collapsed as the Allied forces of England, France, and America started bearing down in a united effort.

As the Americans moved to take the pressure off exhausted French and British army units on the front lines, they inevitably made incursions into largely German-speaking territories, where the residents were likely to be resentful of Allied gains. Perhaps that explains the trepidation felt by a young Jewish American soldier, Alex Lurye, as he entered a small German town with his army unit.[1]

When the Jewish Shabbat (Sabbath) approached on a late Friday afternoon, Lurye sought out the Jewish synagogue. There he met a number of people, but the one who showed him the greatest kindness was a young father who identified himself as Herr Rosenau (Mr. Rosenau). The two men, one in German civilian clothing and the other in an American army uniform, spoke together in English. Lurye began to relax.

At the end of the service, Herr Rosenau invited Lurye to return home with him for a traditional Shabbat meal, which included cakes and crackers and a blessing of sanctification. Lurye was pleased to accept the invitation and went to the modest home of his host. There he celebrated Shabbat with the family. He later wrote that he enjoyed the blessings that were pronounced, as well as a delicious kosher meal that included wine and the singing of Shabbat songs. It was an island of serenity in the midst of war that offered a brief reprieve from the violence and deprivation of military life. Having said goodnight, Lurye returned to his unit, which moved out shortly thereafter.

The experience stayed with him. At the end of the war, he returned home to Duluth, Minnesota, to begin civilian life. One day, while thinking about the experience with the Rosenaus, he decided it would be ungrateful of him not to write and thank them. He posted his letter of appreciation, but Herr Rosenau did not respond. Because the letter was not returned as undeliverable, Lurye assumed it had been delivered. He moved on with his life, establishing himself as a successful businessman in his community.

THE NAZIS COME TO POWER

On January 30, 1933, Adolf Hitler was appointed chancellor of Germany, even though his National Socialist (Nazi) Party had won only 30 percent of the popular vote in the election of 1932.

One of the ways Hitler moved the Nazi Party to national prominence was to blame the Jewish people for the economic misery that Germans were suffering in the midst of the Great Depression. He declared that the Jews had subverted the economy for their own gain and were taking unfair profits from their workers. He repeated the idea that Germany had lost the Great War through betrayal by military leaders and powerful Jewish business interests. Because combat had never penetrated into Germany, the average citizen believed the propaganda that Germany was winning the Great War right up until the shocking announcement was made that the Kaiser and other German leaders had accepted a punishing armistice. It seemed impossible that the fortunes of war could have turned so quickly against them. Given the centuries of anti-Semitism in Europe, many were quick to believe that the Jews were behind the German defeat. The truth was that the defeat had nothing to do with the Jewish people but rather the sheer number of Americans entering the war. It was simply impossible for Germany to continue for long. Defeat might not have been imminent, but it was inevitable.

For German Jews, the rise of the Nazis to political dominance was devastating. Ugly propaganda images portrayed the Jews as murderers of Jesus, as loyal to the "Jewish cause" above patriotism to Germany, and as financial exploiters who kept Christian Germans in economic bondage.

The Nazis not only condoned violence against the Jews but perpetrated it. In 1935, discrimination against Jews gained legal authority when the German Bundestag passed the Nuremberg laws, which mandated the physical separation of Aryan (Germanic) persons from non-Aryan (all others, especially Jewish) persons in all public places. Civil liberties were suspended of those deemed Jewish because of their ancestry rather than religious affiliation. On November 9, 1938, Nazis throughout Germany smashed the windows of synagogues and Jewish businesses and set many on fire. This night became known as *Kristallnacht*, "night of broken glass."

German Jews were suddenly strangers in the land of their birth, but that was only the beginning. It quickly became much worse. After the invasion of Poland in September 1939, the Nazis implemented a program of mass murder aimed at the entire Jewish race.

THE ROSENAUS AND THE LETTER

One day, before the Jewish world descended fully into chaos, Herr Rosenau was tending his young grandson. Rummaging through his grandfather's desk, the boy came across the letter that Alex Lurye had written at the end of World War I. It had an American stamp on the envelope, so the boy asked if he could have it. Not thinking much about it, Rosenau said yes.

When he returned home, the boy showed the letter to his mother. Now grown up with a family of her own, Ruth Wienberg had been a young woman when her family shared their Shabbat dinner with Alex Lurye two decades earlier. As she opened the envelope and read the message of gratitude, the memory of that dinner came back to her. She shared it with her husband, and they talked about the experience.

Somewhere in the conversation, the idea came up that they should write to Alex Lurye. And, even though it was presumptuous, they wondered if he would sponsor them to emigrate to America. The Wienbergs knew that the ill treatment of Jews was likely to get worse, and they yearned to find a place that would accept them. But the laws of the United States restricted foreign immigration unless an American sponsor agreed to accept responsibility for helping immigrants get established in their new country. Not knowing anyone else who might help them, the Weinbergs decided to ask Alex Lurye.

The problem was there was no return address on the letter. Undaunted, they wrote to Lurye, thanking him for writing to Ruth's father twenty years earlier. They also wrote, "We have no future in Germany. We must get out before this madman, Hitler, begins to do worse things to the Jews." Placing their letter in an envelope, they addressed it to "Alex Lurye, Duluth, Minnesota."

The chances of such a letter finding its recipient were slim indeed. The greater Duluth area had a population of approximately 100,000 people. But Alex Lurye had become a successful businessman in Duluth as proprietor of Alex J. Lurye's Fine Furniture store. That was enough of a clue for the United States Post Office to deliver the Wienbergs' letter.

Lurye quickly wrote back with a pledge to help the family immigrate to Duluth. He was as good as his word. In May 1938 the Wienbergs arrived in America. Shortly after that, the Rosenau family joined them.

CAST THY BREAD UPON THE WATERS

Life in America had its challenges, but the family was safe from the Holocaust that took the lives of so many of their Jewish friends and neighbors—and all because of a letter conveying Alex

Lurye's appreciation and gratitude. It would have been easy to let the memory of that one night in Germany slip away. Certainly, Herr Rosenau had shown *chesed* (Hebrew, "loving kindness") to the young American soldier in the last days of World War I. He did it without any thought of future reward. And yet the lives of those who mattered most to him were saved quite literally because of his small gesture.

The story of Herr Rosenau and Alex Lurye exemplifies the Jewish tradition articulated in Ecclesiastes 11:1—"Cast thy bread upon the waters: for thou shalt find it after many days."

CHAPTER 8

RUDOLF WOBBE

SAVED BY A NAZI PRISON GUARD

Three German boys dared to defy Adolf Hitler and the mighty National Socialist (Nazi) Party in the midst of World War II. They were convicted of treason for their actions, their leader sentenced to death by guillotine and the others to hard labor. Three years later, in the last days of the war, the surviving members of the group were given a chance to redeem themselves in the eyes of the Nazis by serving in the army at the front. One accepted the offer, but the other, Rudolf (Rudi) Wobbe, defiantly said that if he had refused to serve Hitler while the Nazis were winning the war, he certainly would not do so when they were losing. The SS recruiter was so infuriated by this bold defiance that he raised his pistol and took aim at Rudi.

THE HUEBENER GROUP—
"PREPARATION TO HIGH TREASON"

In the midst of the twelve-year nightmare of Nazi rule (1933 to 1945), three young Germans had the courage to stand up for freedom. Eventually called the Huebener group, these young men secretly wrote and distributed pamphlets that warned their neighbors in Hamburg about the evil truth behind Adolf Hitler and his national socialist regime. Discovered by the Gestapo in 1942, the three were arrested and brought to trial on the charge of preparation to high treason. Their case was heard by the infamous *Volksgerichtshof* ("the people's court"). Nicknamed the Blood Tribunal, the justices of this court had supreme power. Their charge was to ruthlessly suppress internal dissent, and the three teenagers from Hamburg felt the devastating consequences of the court's unfettered power.

They were tortured by the Gestapo and then, in a sham trial in which no defense was put forward in their behalf, Helmuth Huebener, the seventeen-year-old leader of the group, was sentenced to die by guillotine. His best friend, Rudi Wobbe, was sentenced to ten years at hard labor. Another friend, Karl-Heinz Schnibbe, received a shorter sentence of five years because of his lesser role in the group.

Few people were willing to stand up for these young men for fear they might also be implicated. Their only hope of reprieve was clemency from Adolf Hitler. He refused.

THE PASSION OF YOUTH

The three principal members of this small resistance group were Helmuth Huebener, Rudi Wobbe, and Karl-Heinz Schnibbe, three ordinary boys who grew up in Nazi Germany. Like their schoolmates, they learned the essential details of Nazi life, including the birthdate of the Führer, Adolf Hitler (April 20, 1889); the number of points in the Nazi Party Platform (twenty-five); and the proper respect they should show for their nation. The doctrine of *Gemeinnutz Geht Vor Eigennutz* ("the common good is to be placed above an individual's requirement") penetrated every organization they belonged to, including the Hitler Youth. It was drilled into every German child at school, at play, and even in church. For most people it became the only right way to think—whatever the Nazi Party declared to be true was simply true. Whatever sacrifice the party demanded, the citizens should make.

But Rudi, Helmuth, and Karl-Heinz had something in common that others didn't. Their perceptions of reality were influenced by the world outside Germany. Because of this, they saw past the state-sponsored propaganda that blinded others. Rudi was particularly offended by the Nazis' belief in their racial superiority, which prompted the awful treatment of his Jewish neighbors:

> Near our home was a shoe store, owned and run by a Jew. Even before 1933 his store windows had been broken and swastikas painted on the walls and door. But after the Nazis came to official power they demolished his store in broad daylight. They broke all the windows, threw the merchandise onto the sidewalk, and dragged the proprietor and his wife and two children into the street. They started beating and cursing them, all the while calling them dirty names and shouting that they weren't fit to live among the exalted German Aryan people. The greatest indignity of all is that after the family was lying in the gutter in agony, the Nazis urinated on them. I was only seven years of age when this took place, but I still remember it vividly.[1]

Helmuth Huebener, later judged by the Blood Tribunal to have a genius-level IQ, was incensed by the political oppression of the common people of Germany. For example, Heinrich Worbs, an older member of Helmuth's and Rudi's church congregation, paid a terrible price for speaking his mind. Rudi wrote:

> We learned about the horrors of the Concentration Camp firsthand from our old friend Heinrich Worbs. A simple but honest man, his only fault was that he always said what he was thinking. . . . While watching the Nazis erect a statue of one of their "Nazi heroes," Heinrich remarked, "Another statue to a Nazi butcher!" He was overheard and reported to the Gestapo, which immediately arrested him and shipped him to Neuengamme Concentration Camp for six months. He showed up at church the day after his release, but we could hardly recognize him. He was a broken man, a shadow of his former self. . . .
>
> Six weeks later he died, unable to recover from the ordeal. What upset us the most was the way the other members of our congregation treated him. Rather than rally to his defense to comfort him, many turned a cold shoulder, refusing even to speak with him. He was ostracized because he opposed the government. Many, I suspect, were afraid to be seen with him for fear the Nazis would suspect them as well. This is how the mighty party enforced its iron hold on the citizens. By crushing one man, they could terrify everyone else into quiet submission.[2]

Helmuth was angry for many weeks about the treatment of his friend. In time, he came to believe that Hitler was an anti-Christ who acted against true religion. He concluded that God could not be on the side of the German people and that their war against freedom was doomed to failure. Nor, he believed, could God support a people whose leaders lied to keep them in ignorance.

Despite the danger, Helmuth listened to the British Broadcasting

Corporation (BBC) German language news program on a short-wave radio hidden in his bedroom. He learned through these broadcasts that the German government was lying to its own citizens, and he resolved to do something about it.

BROCHURES BECOME WARRANTS
FOR THEIR ARREST

Skilled in shorthand, Helmuth took notes as he listened to the broadcasts and then used carbon paper to type multiple copies in full and half-page flyers. Rudi and Karl-Heinz surreptitiously distributed these flyers in the working class neighborhoods of Hamburg. The boys were quite ingenious in getting the word out. For example, Rudi sneaked into the Hamburg Opera House and slipped copies into the overcoat pockets of patrons while they were listening to the program. They even posted copies of the flyers on official bulletin boards of the Nazi Party. Because Helmuth put a swastika on most of the flyers, an unsuspecting reader would step up to the board and start reading, only to discover that it was anti-government in nature.

In the end, Helmuth created, and Rudi and Karl-Heinz distributed, more than twenty such flyers. The titles were provocative, including "Hitler Is Guilty of the Bombing Raids over Germany" and "Hitler the Murderer of General von Schroeder of Serbia." Remarkably, no one in the neighborhoods where these brochures were distributed reported them to the authorities.

But one of Helmuth's coworkers became suspicious when he saw Helmuth whispering to another man in the office where they worked as clerks. This man, a spy for the Nazi Party, reported Helmuth to the Gestapo. They quickly connected Helmuth to the offending leaflets and arrested him.

The next ten days were miserable for Rudi and Karl-Heinz as they feared that Helmuth would be tortured into breaking their common vow not to report the others if captured. In any case,

Karl-Heinz was eventually arrested, and then Rudi. The short-lived resistance effort of the Huebener group was at an end. Soon they were to face the justices of the supreme court of Nazi Germany as traitors to their country.

CONVICTED AND SENTENCED

> *Tuesday, 11 August 1942:* All too soon the huge doors in the back of the courtroom swung open and the justices of the Blood Tribunal started to file in. I understood in an instant why they were called the Blood Tribunal. Each justice was dressed in a brilliant crimson robe, the color of blood. . . . They also wore blood-red caps. I can't describe the feeling of horror that this brought upon me. My life was in the hands of these powerful men—men who did not know the love of God.[3]

The prosecution began with Helmuth Huebener as the leader of the group. They set the stage by providing the judges a copy of a patriotic essay Helmuth wrote at age fifteen to show that he understood what was required of a dutiful German citizen. The chief judge was impressed and said, "If this had been submitted to me by a law school student, I would have given him an A Plus grade."

Next, the prosecutor distributed copies of Helmuth's antigovernment pamphlets. One of them, "Hermann Goering, the Fat Dude," was so clever that the judge had to gavel the court into silence. Goering was the heavy commander of Germany's air force, the Luftwaffe. The other leaflets clearly distressed the justices for their "defeatist" tone, cited in one of the charges leveled against the Huebener group.

The chief judge soon took the lead in questioning Helmuth, sometimes leaving the prosecutor out of the interchange altogether. At one point, the judge asked Helmuth if he believed the enemy propaganda he listened to on his shortwave radio more than he believed the *Wehrmachtsbericht* ("Armed Forces News"). Helmuth replied that he did. When pressed, and perhaps to irritate the judge, Helmuth asked if any of the judges really believed that Germany could win the war. At that point the chief judge lost his composure and screamed at Helmuth, "Silence! How dare you speak that way in my courtroom!"[4]

As the questioning proceeded, it became quite clear to Helmuth that they were going to be convicted, no matter what he said. He intentionally drew the ire of the court to himself to shield the other defendants. This tactic likely saved their lives.

In the end, the court convicted all the defendants of treason. Helmuth Huebener was deprived of all civil rights and was sentenced to death by guillotine. Rudi Wobbe was sentenced to ten years' imprisonment, and Karl-Heinz Schnibbe to five. The sentences were harsher even than the ones recommended by the prosecutor.

Rudi and Helmuth, shocked at the verdict, were taken from the courtroom and placed in a holding cell. Rudi was so overwhelmed at the thought of Helmuth being executed that it was difficult for him to speak to his friend. Finally, he tried to offer some words of comfort, suggesting that perhaps Adolf Hitler would listen to the many appeals for leniency that would likely be put forward in their behalf. But Helmuth knew better. He pointed to graffiti on the wall of the prison cell where previous prisoners had scribbled their fate at the hands of the Blood Tribunal.

"Do you still think they don't mean it, Rudi?" asked Helmuth. "They are all mad with power."

Rudi recalled that just then a guard unlocked the door and called to him, "You are in the wrong cell."

As Rudi stood to leave, he and Helmuth embraced for the last time. "Rudi, live well, and remember me!" were Helmuth's last words to his lifelong friend.

All Rudi could reply was, "Helmuth!"[5]

IMPRISONMENT AND A NEAR DEATH EXCHANGE

After twenty days in Berlin, Rudi and Karl-Heinz were sent to Glasmoor Prison, north of their hometown of Hamburg. There they were assigned to the tailor shop, where they repaired the clothing of prisoners and guards. Rudi became very skilled at this work, perhaps from the dexterity he had developed as an apprentice machinist before his arrest.

No one told them what was happening to their friend Helmuth until the master tailor called them into his room on October 28, 1942. He showed them a news item in the newspaper:

> Helmuth Huebener, Age 17
> From Hamburg
>   Who was sentenced to death on 11 August 1942 by the People's Court for "Preparation to High Treason in Connection with Aiding and Abetting the Enemy," with the deprivation of Civil Rights and Honors for the rest of his life, WAS EXECUTED TODAY!
>   Berlin, 27 October 1942
>   The Attorney General of the People's Court

Rudi records that everyone sobbed at this unhappy news. The shop master offered them time to compose themselves before returning to their duties. Rudi's hopes of clemency for Helmuth from Adolf Hitler were in vain, though it had been requested by the Hitler Youth and even the prosecutor in his trial. The mighty Nazi Party feared a seventeen-year-old boy too much to let him live.

RUDI PUTS HIS LIFE IN JEOPARDY

By early 1945 everyone knew that the war was going badly for the Germans. Word was received that the prisoners were to be sent back to Hamburg, which resulted in a grueling trek through winter storms that nearly cost them their lives. After enduring a harrowing march and a crowded train ride, Rudi and Karl-Heinz were assigned to a prison on Hahnöfersand Island in the middle of the Elbe River in Hamburg. With British and American bombers flying daily missions over Hamburg, Rudi felt that their prison in the middle of the river was like being in the eye of a hurricane, with fury and flames on every side. The Allied forces were advancing on every front—the Americans from the west, the British from the north, and the Russians from the east—making the Nazis' need for troops increasingly desperate.

To meet this need, recruiters went to the prisons to offer clemency to even the most violent criminals, including murderers and rapists, if they agreed to serve in the army. Many availed themselves of the opportunity to get out of prison. When the offer was extended to Rudi, though, he did not consider it an extension of mercy. Here is how Rudi describes the confrontation:

> After a patriotic speech by the recruiting officer, we were told that a special battalion would be created for us and that we would have the honor of going to the hottest part of the front line where we could fight the enemy and contribute to the glorious end-victory for Germany. This noble action would restore to us all our rights and honors as citizens so we could start postwar life with a clean slate. It sounded grand and patriotic, but I wasn't impressed. I'd heard of these rehabilitation units and knew that they were nothing more than cannon fodder to be placed in front of the regular troops. . . . Their real purpose was to dig trenches for the soldiers that would follow.

I didn't want any part of this great opportunity and decided to refuse the offer.

"It's because of you that I have had to survive this ordeal for the past three years," I said to the recruiter. "I didn't join the Army when Germany was winning the war, so I certainly won't do you any favors now that the war is almost lost."

That was the wrong thing to say to an overzealous recruiting officer; he pulled out his pistol and started squealing like a stuck pig. In a shrill voice he screamed "What do you mean, that the war is almost lost? The victory is in sight and we haven't even shown them the Führer's secret weapon yet—one so terrible that it will destroy the enemy forever. You are a defeatist and I should shoot you right now, you Schweinehund!" With that, he pointed his pistol directly at my head. I thought it was the end.[6]

A MOMENT OF COURAGE AND MERCY

The other prisoners and the guards near Rudi shied away as the SS recruiter stepped forward to shoot him. Though the prisoners did not wish to infuriate the recruiter, the prison guards were older men who were not physically able to serve in the army. They had families, dreams, and hopes for the future. Millions of people had died in the war, and one more death of a defiant teenager would mean nothing in the overall scheme of things. The prudent thing to do for everyone in that room was to let the terrible scene unfold with Rudi dying at the hands of the SS recruiter. It is certain that there would have been no repercussions to anyone, including the recruiter and the guards. Quite simply, no one was keeping track of prison deaths anymore.

But that isn't what happened. In that moment, one brave guard decided to protect Rudi—to give him his future:

Much to my surprise and relief, however, one of the prison guards stepped directly in front of me and said to the infuriated officer as calmly as he could, "Do not take him too seriously; he is sick in the head and does not know what he is saying."

With that the guard, Mr. Pape, stepped back and moved me to the side, out of the line of fire.[7]

The SS recruiter was surprised enough by this action that he lowered his gun and turned to the rest of the group to continue his recruiting effort. Most of the men raised their hands to say they would accept the offer, including Karl-Heinz Schnibbe. After all, they had witnessed firsthand what could happen if they refused, and Mr. Pape's brave strategy would only work once.

Once Rudi was no longer the focus of attention, Mr. Pape removed him from danger:

After dragging me from the room he gave me a tongue-lashing of his own. "Are you crazy, man?" he asked. "Just what did you think you were doing in there? Are you tired of living?"

I was still in shock from the terror of looking into the barrel of a loaded gun held by a maniac. After I had come back to my senses, I thanked Mr. Pape for saving my life. It took great courage for him to step in front of that gun to protect me.[8]

That is how Rudi Wobbe's life was saved. The SS recruiter was one of the elite German boys who had been taken from their parents at a young age to be raised and tutored as Hitler's attack dogs. These men were fanatical in their loyalty to Hitler and his regime, and they took precedence over regular army officers.

For Rudi to insult one of these men was extremely dangerous but very much in character. He had little regard for authority before he was captured, but he was powerless in this situation. His defiance toward the SS recruiter would have been fatal had it not been for the Nazi guard. To interrupt a scene unfolding so quickly put Mr. Pape's life at risk as well, and yet he ran that risk to save a defiant young man who had a lot of life left to live.

AFTER THE WAR

The war ended, Rudi was set free to return to his home in Hamburg, and he was reunited with his family. He eventually married, had a child, and then immigrated to the United States, where he became a naturalized citizen.

Many years after the war, in 1985, Rudi and Karl-Heinz, who had also immigrated to the States, were invited to return to Hamburg to join in a number of events honoring the memory of Helmuth Huebener. On what would have been Helmuth's sixtieth birthday, January 8 of that year, a memorial service was held by the Hamburg state senate to honor the boys who once had been found guilty of treason but were now honored as heroes of the resistance. Helmuth was the youngest person to be executed by the Nazis.

Rudi and Karl-Heinz were awarded the German medal of honor "for outstanding merits in the fight against the national socialistic tyranny and the reestablishment of freedom and democracy." The award was presented by the VVN, an organization created for the victims of Nazi injustice. This was one of many awards granted to Helmuth posthumously and in life to Rudi and Karl-Heinz.

For many years, Rudi did not speak of the war, but he never forgot his friend Helmuth Huebener, whom he idolized, nor the guard who had risked his life to save Rudi's.

CHAPTER 9

DIETRICH VON CHOLTITZ
NINETEEN DAYS IN PARIS

Ass a field commander in the long Nazi siege of the Soviet port city of Sevastopol, Ukraine, Major General Dietrich von Choltitz showed no remorse in conquering the city in July 1942. Born to a long line of Prussian military officers, he believed that orders given are orders to be obeyed, even if it meant inflicting incredible suffering. So fierce was his loyalty to Adolf Hitler that von Choltitz drove his 4,800-man regiment to the brink of destruction. More than 4,400 of them were killed before the city was taken, and he was wounded—all for an occupation that lasted less than two years. When the Germans withdrew from Sevastopol in May 1944, von Choltitz assisted in the scorched earth policy that left the city in total ruin—a smoldering mass of twisted rebar and rubble.

Because of his undoubted loyalty to his Führer, it was to von

Choltitz that Hitler turned later in 1944 when he wanted to destroy another city. Von Choltitz had had a heavy hand in the devastation of Sevastopol. Would he be able to inflict the same to a city with far greater population and cultural significance?

THE ALLIES INVADE FRANCE IN 1944

With the successful Allied landings at Normandy on D-Day, the Nazis faced an ever-increasing tide of Allied troops and artillery forcing their way east towards the Rhine River and the German homeland. The Allies advanced on three fronts—the north, the west, and the south. From a military point of view, the most effective way to keep the advance moving was to bypass the city of Paris and link the three Allied armies east of the city. That would cut supply lines from Germany to the more than 20,000 occupiers of Paris. Without the need for hand-to-hand combat in the heavily populated city, the Allies could maintain their momentum. That was exactly the battle plan created by General Dwight D. Eisenhower, commander of the Allied forces in Europe.

But Eisenhower hadn't counted on two things. First was the political maneuvering of General Charles de Gaulle, leader of the Free French forces who had been driven to North Africa by the Nazis at the beginning of the war. De Gaulle was determined to return to Paris to establish himself as the leader of France before Communists in the city could assume control. Second was Adolf Hitler's fanatical determination to either hold Paris or burn it to the ground. This was not an idle threat. On the Eastern Front, Warsaw was even then under heavy bombardment that completely devastated the city. The German assault on Warsaw took place despite the fact that the bombs and troops used to raze the Polish city could have been used more effectively against the advancing Russians in the east or the Americans and British in the west.

But the Jews in Warsaw had had the temerity to rise up against their Nazi tormentors, and so Hitler spared no expense in punishing them, even though it served no military purpose. By this time the great Führer, head of the German Third Reich, was a vindictive and bitter man. Just two months earlier several of his senior officers had attempted to assassinate him by planting a bomb under a table where he stood. When the bomb exploded, the table saved his life but left him wounded and hard of hearing. Now, with the Allied landings in western France, he stood to lose Paris, his most cherished conquest. Here is what he had to say:

> If we are to hold the Seine, we must hold Paris. We will hold in front of Paris, we will hold in Paris, we will hold Paris. . . . I want all the Seine bridges in the Paris area mined and prepared for destruction. . . . Industry must be paralyzed. . . . Paris is to be defended to the last man without regard for the destruction the fighting may cause. Why should we care if Paris is destroyed? The Allies, at this very moment, are destroying cities all over Germany with their bombs.[1]

As this Nazi strategy became clear, it seemed unthinkable that Eisenhower would leave the more than three million residents of the city unprotected from Nazi reprisals when three Allied army groups were close enough to render aid.

The stage was set for what might have turned into a human tragedy of epic proportions. Some estimates put the expected number of casualties from street warfare in Paris at more than 200,000. Plus, the Allied assault would result in the Germans' destroying all gasworks, railroads, electric generation facilities, and bridges in Paris. Their goal was to destroy the infrastructure of the city and leave the citizens to freeze and starve during the approaching winter.

From a military point of view, the German strategy would transfer the burden of feeding Parisians to the Allies and bog down their military advance. Such a strategy was understandable in all-out war. But Hitler's disdain for the cultural treasures of the ancient city, including the museums, the Eiffel Tower, the universities, and galleries, seemed much less justifiable. His planned actions served no military purpose and diverted ordnance and munitions that could have been used to protect Germany. It was a foolish as well as vindictive use of resources. But Adolf Hitler was determined that if he lost the crown jewel of his earliest military success, then he would destroy the city in retribution.

THE CITY OF LIGHT

Paris became known as the City of Light for its central role in the Age of Enlightenment, the intellectual awakening that advanced science and reason in the eighteenth century. But in living up to its name, Paris had also turned itself into a city of lights by illuminating more than 250 public buildings and promenades after the invention of the electric lightbulb. Before World War II, the city glittered at night with thousands of lights shining on the Eiffel Tower as well as floodlights brilliantly illuminating such magnificent buildings as the Paris Opera House, the Louvre Museum in the gardens of the Tuileries, and others. For more than two thousand years Paris had stood as the center of culture and refinement in the Western world. Now it faced extinction.

Hitler despised Paris. He viewed it as the place of Germany's great humiliation at the end of World War I when France and Britain forced German leaders to sign the Treaty of Versailles in the suburbs of Paris. The treaty assigned all blame for the war to Germany, even though all the European nations involved had been eager to meet on the field of battle. Against advice from the United States, Britain and France were determined to punish Germany and used the treaty to strip Germany of her empire. War reparations impoverished the Germans and set the stage for the rise of Nazism.

Many Americans believe that Hitler achieved his power through a combination of brute force and political maneuvering. Indeed, that was how he gained the office of chancellor of the Weimar Republic. But afterward he was elected by overwhelming majorities because of his fiery rhetoric denouncing the French and English while calling for a glorious rebirth of Germany as the savior of depressed Europe. Once firmly in power, he moved quietly and in violation of the Treaty of Versailles to rebuild the German military until it was the most potent military force in the world.

On September 1, 1939, Germany launched World War II by invading Poland. The next year, in just a matter of weeks, the Germans completely overwhelmed France, driving their way quickly to Paris. In his moment of triumph and at the height of his military power, Hitler forced the French to sign a document of surrender in the very same railroad car where German leaders had signed the despised Treaty of Versailles two decades earlier. Then he blew up the railroad car! He planned for the vanquished citizens of Paris to live under German occupation for at least the thousand years of his new Third Reich ("kingdom"). He considered the conquest of Paris among his greatest accomplishments in redeeming German honor.

Four years later, in August 1944, the City of Light was dark—its people deprived of fuel and facing starvation. It made no sense for the Germans to continue to hold Paris while the Allies pressed toward Germany. Yet Adolf Hitler could not stand the thought of losing the city, and if he did, he would destroy it once and for all.

A CITY READY TO FIGHT

General Dietrich von Choltitz, after three years on the Eastern Front, was summoned to Berlin to meet Adolf Hitler and his military chief of staff, General Alfred Jodl. Although von Choltitz had always held Adolf Hitler in the highest regard, he found him angry and confused at this meeting. Hitler's injuries from the failed assassination had caused a noticeable deterioration in his health and mental acuity. Still, Hitler made it clear that von Choltitz was to defend Paris to the last man, without regard for injury to civilians or historical or cultural sites. If the Allies appeared to be gaining the upper hand, then von Choltitz was to destroy the city. Still believing there was a military purpose to his assignment and seeing no point in crossing Hitler, the general accepted his new command and made his way to France.

Arriving in the city August 8, 1944, von Choltitz quickly figured out that he had many problems to deal with. First, the German troops stationed in Paris were soft and pampered. Many had been there since the beginning of the war, and their discipline contrasted sharply with that of the battle-hardened soldiers in the harsh conditions von Choltitz had endured with them on the Eastern Front. Second, the citizens of Paris were anxious to be liberated—they knew full well that the Allies had landed in Normandy and were making rapid military progress against the Germans. Nearly everyone in Paris believed their liberation was imminent. Third, and perhaps most important, many Parisians wanted to be part of liberating their city. They felt shame for the suddenness of their defeat in 1940. After four years of covertly resisting German occupation, both the Communists and the Gaullists were eager to more openly harass the Germans and force the conflict of liberation. These two groups believed that the group that acted first would gain the advantage in assuming postwar leadership.

But now the Parisians faced the new reality of General von Choltitz's leadership. He replaced Generalfeldmarschall Hugo Sperlle as military governor of Paris. Sperlle had relished his four years in Paris. While Germans were being killed on battlefields in Africa, Russia, Italy, the Baltic states, and the Crimea, Sperlle and his officers dressed for a formal dinner each night, often at the magnificent Palais du Luxembourg. He and many of the 25,000 Germans assigned to his command shared Hitler's dream of a German occupation of Paris lasting a thousand years—but mostly for their own comfort and convenience. Now that dream was threatened, and Sperrle was forced out.

Von Choltitz quickly showed his disdain for the luxurious lifestyle of his predecessor. He moved out of the palace into more austere quarters. Candlelit formal dinners for the military staff were ended. The German-language movies at the Opera House were no more. He made it clear to the Parisians that their German conquerors were preparing for combat with the Allies.

Two munitions engineers from Germany arrived in Paris specifically to prepare the city for destruction, and von Choltitz gave orders to proceed with the strategic placement of explosives throughout the city. Priority was given to electric, gas, and waterworks, so that when the order to detonate was given, the city would be paralyzed. Explosives were also placed under all the Seine River bridges to slow the Allies' advance into the city. More ominous was the filling of one of the many tunnels under the heart of the city with a huge cache of submarine torpedoes from a manufacturing plant that had supplied U-Boats with torpedoes earlier in the war. Blasting caps were placed strategically throughout the stockpile, so the Nazis could destroy the center of the city in one huge, spectacular explosion. All von Choltitz had to do was give the order.

But the general hesitated, mostly for practical reasons. Addressing the men who had prepared the city for destruction, he subdued their eagerness to proceed by reminding them of his primary goal: defend the city from Allied attack while keeping German soldiers alive and supplied. It made no sense, he declared, to destroy the city until it was clear that the Germans were ready to evacuate it.

Soon after von Choltitz delayed the order to proceed, he received a telegram from his superior officer, Feldmarschall Gunter von Kluge. It read: "I give the order for the neutralization and destruction envisaged for Paris."[2] Von Choltitz set the order aside, explaining to von Kluge that the required ordnance work was not yet ready.

That was only partly true. Though it did not make sense to destroy the infrastructure of the city while the Nazis still occupied it, he could have issued orders to destroy the railroad stations, aircraft factories, and other large manufacturing facilities that could be used against the Germans if they fell into Allied hands. Yet von Choltitz hesitated. It was the first of his deceptions to his superior officers to delay setting the city aflame.

Perhaps a conversation with the mayor of Paris, Pierre Charles Taittinger, had something to do with the military governor's hesitation. Earlier that day the mayor had called on von Choltitz to express anxiety about all the bombs being placed throughout the city. He asked the general why that was being done.

The reply was chilling. Von Choltitz pointed to a map of Paris and said casually, "Suppose a bullet is fired at one of my soldiers, here, on the avenue de l'Opera. I would burn down every building in the block, and shoot down their inhabitants." He had "22,000 troops, mostly SS, a hundred Tiger tanks, and ninety aircraft" to carry out such reprisals. "As an officer, Mr. Taittinger, you will understand there are certain measures which I shall have to take in Paris. It is my duty to slow up as much as possible the advance of the Allies." Taittinger later said that he thought at the time, "This man was preparing to destroy Paris as indifferently as if it were a crossroads village in the Ukraine."[3]

What could the mayor of Paris do? As a collaborator with the Nazis for the past four years, Taittinger knew he would be treated with contempt by his French compatriots once the city was retaken by either de Gaulle or the Communists, perhaps even tried for treason. Until now, he had had little reason to oppose the Nazis, but the vision of Paris destroyed was unthinkable to him. He needed to be bold.

As Taittinger and von Choltitz stepped onto a balcony overlooking the gardens of the Tuileries and beyond them to the incomparable Louvre Museum, Taittinger said quietly to his German superior,

> "Often it is given to a general to destroy, rarely to preserve. Imagine that one day it may be given you to stand on this balcony again, as a tourist, to look once more on these monuments to our joys, to our sufferings, and be able to say, 'One day I could have destroyed this, and I preserved it as a gift to humanity.' General, is not that worth all a conqueror's glory?"
>
> Von Choltitz was moved but still replied, "You are a good advocate for Paris, Monsieur Taittinger. You have done your duty well. Likewise I, as a German general, must do mine."[4]

INSURRECTION AND A FAILED TRUCE

Events quickly forced von Choltitz to move. On August 19, General de Gaulle's handpicked leaders in Paris beat the Communists to the punch by ordering resistance fighters to attack German positions throughout the city. The Communists were angry to be outmaneuvered but quickly joined in the fighting, adding their 25,000 combatants to the fray. The shared goal of the Gaullists and the Communists was to force Eisenhower to change his plans. But Eisenhower was not easily moved. In spite of repeated appeals, he stuck to his original battle plan.

In Paris, von Choltitz immediately recognized the danger of the uprising and prepared to attack the main point of resistance, the police headquarters, with aircraft of the Luftwaffe. It would be an easy thing for the Germans to destroy the building with bombs while killing the resistance leaders and fighters who had taken the building hostage. But at this critical moment another person intervened to try to save Paris—Raoul Nordling, the Swedish consul in France. Nordling proposed that he negotiate a ceasefire between the parties so they could recover their wounded and dead. He recognized that the resistance was failing in the face of the superior power of the German occupiers, so he felt that they would be open to negotiation. For his part, von Choltitz recognized that the reinforcements he had been promised had not yet been dispatched and that the destruction of the police building would incite the Parisians to even more action. So he agreed, and Nordling successfully negotiated a truce.

The truce lasted for just a few days before the Communists started new attacks. But it was a critical few days. Then the Communists blackmailed the Gaullists back into the fray by threatening to put up posters all over the city accusing de Gaulle of stabbing the people of Paris in the back through this ceasefire. Once again, von Choltitz was faced with insurrection.

TREASON

Fortunately, two events now transpired to help Paris. First was that General Jacques Philippe Leclerc of the 2d Free French Armored Division, under the command of General Eisenhower but loyal to de Gaulle, was preparing to withdraw from the Allied Expeditionary Force and to march directly to Paris on his own authority. The second was an incredible encounter between General von Choltitz and Raoul Nordling. As the ceasefire collapsed around him, von Choltitz asked the ambassador to meet him at his headquarters. After some uneasy small talk, von Choltitz told Nordling that he had received a number of orders over the previous days to begin the destruction of Paris—orders that he had not yet followed. He said that he had delayed because he hoped that Nordling's ceasefire would reestablish peace in the city, but now that it had failed, he would have to act very soon or be relieved of his command. Here is what happened next:

Speaking slowly and in a very somber tone, von Choltitz leaned forward and told Nordling that the only thing that might prevent those orders from being carried out was the rapid arrival of the Allies in Paris. Wheezing slightly with asthma, he added, his voice faint, "You must realize that my behavior in telling you this could be interpreted as treason." For a few seconds the room was still and breathless in the warm August midday. Then, choosing his words very carefully, von Choltitz spoke a final phrase: "Because," he said, "what I am really doing is asking the Allies to help me." Nordling felt the impact of each one of von Choltitz's words.[5]

That was the moment when Dietrich von Choltitz, a loyal German officer, decided to try to save Paris from destruction. It was a personally dangerous decision to make. If this conversation became known, von Choltitz could be tried and executed as a traitor. Worse, his family was also at risk. After the attempted assassination of Hitler, the Nazi high command had made it known that any officer found guilty of acting against the Führer would be forced to witness the arrest and execution of all members of his immediate family. Von Choltitz was a devoted family man with a wife and two daughters. In having this conversation with Nordling and delaying obedience to direct orders to destroy Paris, von Choltitz was committing treason against the Third Reich. But in protecting the great city of Paris from destruction, he was also attempting to save the lives of hundreds of thousands of Parisians.

EISENHOWER RELENTS

Raoul Nordling next undertook one of his most hazardous operations of the war. He had to make his way through German checkpoints to take the remarkable message to the Allies. That meant he had to find and meet with the highest levels of Allied command and persuade them that he was actually speaking for the German commander of Gross Paris. It seemed impossible. Then, as he was making last-minute preparations for his car trip out of Paris, he learned that he was to be joined by a number of others, men who were dispatched by von Choltitz to add credibility and authority to the mission. These included a Red Cross official, who also happened to be the underground leader of the French resistance for the past four years, as well as a high-ranking German officer who was also a secret agent for the Allies.

When they finally reached General Omar Bradley of the American army, Nordling was exhausted. But he conveyed his message and added the desperate plea that the Allies move immediately. Von Choltitz had told him that the longest he could delay taking action was 48 hours, and 24 had already been used in getting through the Allied lines. Bradley was astounded by Nordling's message. Von Choltitz had intimated that for a brief moment there was a clear and open path to Paris because German reinforcements had not yet started to move. The message also indicated that von Choltitz would hold off destroying the city. If the Allies acted quickly, they could get through to the city with almost no resistance.

Nordling feared that it would take time for Bradley to communicate with Eisenhower and receive permission to change the battle plan. What he didn't know was that Eisenhower had already decided to liberate Paris on his own. While Eisenhower was frustrated at having to divert critical troops and supplies away from the advance on the Rhine, he realized that history would never forgive him or the Allies if they failed to protect the great city of Paris at this crucial moment. Eisenhower had already given Bradley authority to dispatch the 2d Free French Armored to Paris under the command of General Leclerc.

Now Bradley moved with far greater haste. "We can't take any chances on that general changing his mind and knocking the hell out of the city," he said.[6] He added additional firepower by diverting the 4th Division towards Paris as it was geographically closer.

The race was now on. The Free French fighters made it to Paris first, followed quickly by a wave of Americans. At any point during the Allied advance, von Choltitz and his subordinates could have blown up the bridges, landmarks, factories, and communication exchanges. The railroads, the gas lines, and the electric generation plants were all vulnerable. Yet von Choltitz withheld his authorization, and no German took independent action to put the city in flames. By this time the phone lines and telegraph lines were melting from the fury of Adolf Hitler, Jodl, and von Kluge, who all repeated over and over the command to destroy the city. It was already too late to defend it; there simply weren't enough German troops and tanks to move to the city. It was not too late to inflict some Nazi venom on the city, however.

Yet the scourge of Sevastopol and the destroyer of Rotterdam, General Dietrich von Choltitz, had made up his mind. He had always acted to further German military aims, but he would not destroy Paris to appease the vindictiveness of Adolf Hitler. Von Choltitz later said that he was convinced by this time that Hitler was insane, driven there by his military reverses and the injuries received in the assassination attempt on his life. Von Choltitz felt a far greater commitment to humanity than he did to a madman.

PARIS STILL AT RISK

On August 25, 1944, General von Choltitz surrendered to Lieutenant Henri Karcher of the army of General de Gaulle. Von Choltitz was nearly killed by angry Parisians as the motorcade taking him to prison made its way through the Paris streets. Even though he'd been there just nineteen days, the Parisians held him responsible for all the German atrocities of the previous four years. Not until after the end of the war would the people of Paris learn the truth about von Choltitz's risking his life and those of his family by failing to destroy Paris.

Dietrich von Choltitz was made a prisoner of war and sent to England. In Germany a trial in absentia was begun by the Nazis to try von Choltitz for treason. Fortunately for von Choltitz and his family, he had enough supporters in Berlin to delay the proceedings until the war ended. This tactic saved the wife and children of von Choltitz from imprisonment and perhaps execution. General von Choltitz was held by the Allies until 1947, first in England and then in Mississippi. He was eventually released without charges and allowed to return to his home in Baden-Baden. Though appreciated by the French, he was sometimes snubbed by former military comrades who considered his failure to act against Paris an act of insubordination.

A PROPHECY FULFILLED

In 1956 Dietrich von Choltitz returned to Paris and made his way to the Hotel Meurice, which had been his headquarters for the nineteen days he had spent as military governor of the city in 1944. The manager of the hotel recognized the general and spoke with him. Von Choltitz asked if he could see the room from which he had commanded the city twelve years earlier.

The manager complied, since it was now well known to everyone in France what von Choltitz had done to save the city. He spent just fifteen minutes in the room, including a few moments on the balcony that overlooks the gardens of the Tuileries. The Place de la Concorde was to his right, as was the Eiffel Tower. Visitors strolled through the gardens while lines queued to enter the Louvre Museum beyond. Perhaps he remembered the words of the mayor of Paris spoken on that same balcony not many years before.

Dietrich von Choltitz died in 1966. Now, nearly three-quarters of a century later, the City of Light continues to shine as a consequence of one man's compassion and bravery.

CHAPTER 10

ROBERT SHEEKS

SAVING ENEMY CIVILIANS AND SOLDIERS IN THE PACIFIC

Because of his experiences growing up in Shanghai, China, Lieutenant Robert Sheeks had been embittered toward the Japanese in World War II. Yet, at the end of the war, he was commended by the United States Marine Corps for saving many Japanese lives.

To be clear, saving *American* lives was the motive of the United States Army in training Sheeks and others in his unit to encourage Japanese soldiers and civilians to surrender rather than fight on to their deaths or to commit suicide. One of the highest-risk assignments an American soldier faced during the war in the Pacific was seeking out pockets of Japanese survivors on the islands where major battles had taken place. Coming from a culture in which surrender was considered treason and even blasphemy against their emperor, the Japanese fought ferociously to kill as many Americans as possible, even when victory was impossible.

It was in this environment that Lieutenant Robert Sheeks was to make his mark on world history. To his great surprise, he ended up saving many hundreds of Japanese lives. His unique role led to his becoming one of the few people in world history to receive formal commendations for saving *enemy* lives. It was an act of humanity by Bob Sheeks as an individual and by the United States military in which he served. With dauntless courage and resolve, he overcame prejudice to show compassion in extreme circumstances.

SHEEKS'S PREWAR WORLDVIEW

Having grown up in Shanghai, China, as the sons of a successful American businessman, Bob Sheeks and his brother were there when the Japanese invaded Manchuria in 1931. Their rather idyllic life in a quiet expatriate section of the ancient Chinese city was disrupted when the family was forced by the invasion to move into a protected enclave in downtown Shanghai. This put them farther from school and friends and closer to the palpable anxiety of city residents.

There they saw firsthand the cruelty with which the Japanese conquerors treated the Chinese people. For example, Bob's father took him and his older brother to the abandoned home of a British family they'd been friends with. The British family had decided that it was simply too dangerous in China and so had moved to Hong Kong a few days earlier. When they arrived at the home, Bob and his father and brother were stunned to see the havoc wreaked upon it by the Japanese invaders. They'd destroyed furniture, damaged walls, and torn down curtains while looking for valuables to steal. When they found nothing, the Japanese invaders murdered the Chinese servants in retribution. They made their deaths as grisly as possible. Two of the servants were grilled alive over an outdoor barbecue pit.

It was a horrifying sight for a child and brought home the reality of all the other violence they witnessed in the city of Bob's birth.[1]

Four years later, in 1935, Bob's father decided to repatriate his family to the United States. Two years after that, the Japanese launched a full-scale invasion of the Chinese mainland. Americans who were still living in China after the attack on Pearl Harbor in 1941 were interned by the occupying Japanese forces. That would have been Bob's fate had his family not left in 1935.

Bob flourished academically in the United States. He quickly adapted to life in America. After graduating from high school, he received a full academic scholarship to Harvard in 1940. Given his interest in the Far East, he made room in his schedule for one Chinese language class and one Chinese history class.

As America's relationship with Japan deteriorated, Bob found himself in many discussions about the Japanese people. These discussions took on increasing urgency after news of the atrocities committed by the Japanese against the Chinese citizens of Nanking became public knowledge. American hatred of Japan grew with each newscast. His college roommate had lived in Japan as a child, and he tried to present a more moderate view of the average Japanese person, but Bob was not persuaded. He said he had come to hate the Japanese and hoped he would have the chance to avenge his Chinese friends if America went to war.

As it turned out, he did not have to wait long. Bob had had just three semesters at Harvard when war broke out in the Pacific. Having joined the Marine Corps Reserves before going to Harvard, he expected to be activated in a combat role. Instead, he received an invitation from the United States Navy to enroll in a Japanese language immersion program at the Berkeley campus of the University of California. Because of Sheeks's life experiences in living in Asia and the fact that both the Chinese and the Japanese use kanji characters with identical meanings, the Navy thought he would be of use in their language and intelligence operations. He accepted the invitation and its promise that he would become a commissioned officer at the end of the training. After completing his final exams at Harvard, Sheeks moved to Berkeley.

JAPAN IN WORLD WAR II

Adolf Hitler believed that the world should be governed by four great world powers: Germany, Britain, the United States, and Japan. He believed that the people of these nations had proved themselves naturally superior to other groups within their respective spheres of influence. Thus, Germany should rule Europe and Russia, Britain her worldwide colonial empire, the United States should predominate in the Western Hemisphere, and Japan should rule all of Asia. The Japanese shared this worldview, at least with respect to Asia. They believed themselves a master race favored by the gods in creation. Indeed, they regarded their emperor as a god incarnate. Almost without exception, a Japanese citizen would willingly sacrifice his or her life for the emperor.

Having remained completely closed to the outside world for more than two hundred years, Japan's isolation was pried open in the early years of the twentieth century by the United States during the presidency of Theodore Roosevelt. Once they opened their ports to the Western world, they quickly showed their resourcefulness in adapting to the modern world. In just a few decades, Japan became an industrial giant whose need for natural resources sent them looking for oil, steel, and other essential raw ingredients to feed their quickly industrialized economy. To them it seemed quite natural to impose a regional hegemony over their Asian neighbors, drawing the resources they needed to strengthen their position as the central power in this part of the world.

Puzzling to them was that America, their first benefactor, became wary of their rapidly expanding influence throughout the Far

East. Rather than stand aside when Japan invaded Korea and China, America aggressively tried to thwart their success by imposing economic embargoes and building up a strong military presence in the Philippines and Hawaii to contain Japan. As the embargo cut deeper and deeper into Japanese expansion, their militaristic leadership felt they had to go to war with the United States to drive them out of Asia. Unlike Hitler, who hoped to conquer and occupy the lands he invaded, the Japanese were primarily interested in simply getting the United States out of the Western Pacific. With abundant natural resources of their own, the Japanese reasoned, the United States would quickly tire of Asia and leave Japan alone. They chose to attack the United States Navy at Pearl Harbor in 1941 because they knew that America was already stretched thin in helping to supply the British and Russians in the European war with Germany.

To their surprise and disappointment, America proved itself more than capable of fighting a two-front war, with major commitments to both Europe and the Pacific. After Japan's quick successes in the opening days of World War II—in which they captured the Philippines, mainland China, Burma, Singapore, and hundreds of South Pacific islands—they were stymied by America's great sea victory at Midway Island in June 1942. After Midway, the United States and Great Britain began to crack open the circle of protection Japan had built around their home islands.

This presented a real dilemma for Japanese soldiers and civilians who lived and fought on these islands. Fierce warriors, they made America pay dearly for every inch of soil recaptured. Indeed, they fought with religious zeal, for they felt it was their individual duty and honor to fight to the end of their life for their divine emperor, and even when death was certain, most Japanese preferred to commit suicide than be taken prisoner of war by the Americans. Author Gerald A. Meehl described this paradigm as follows:

> Japan's leaders emphasized that no member of the
> Japanese military would ever submit to capture, and
> no soldier or sailor could allow himself to be taken
> prisoner and remain alive. If faced with capture, sui-
> cide was mandatory. They could not become prisoners
> and remain Japanese citizens. Japan's military leaders
> also subscribed to the Bushido warrior creed of suicide
> rather than dishonor.[2]

Avoiding at all costs being taken prisoner may have been both a matter of honor and of fear, considering the brutal treatment Japanese guards gave American and Filipino prisoners of war. The Japanese would not want to surrender and face an imprisonment similar to their own. Cruel simply isn't a strong enough word to convey their wretched treatment of prisoners.

JAPANESE IMMERSION AT BERKELEY

On his first day of class after his move to California in 1942, Bob Sheeks was surprised to learn that his instructor was Dr. Nakamura Susumu, chairman of the Japanese language department. The surprise was that he would be taught the Japanese language by Nisei, American-born descendants of Japanese immigrants. In the midst of the war with Japan, it was hard for many Americans to imagine that people who looked so Japanese could be loyal to the United States rather than to their ancestral homeland. Nevertheless, Sheeks was impressed with Dr. Susumu and the other teachers. The course of study was grueling—complete immersion in the Japanese language for one year, with weekly written tests and assignments. If any student fell behind, he would immediately be dismissed from the program and his local draft board informed of his availability. In other words, all hope of receiving a commission as an officer would be lost and a combat role given in its place. The students, then, buckled down to learn the language.[3]

In the course of the next year, Bob found that he really liked his Nisei instructors. Most were children of Japanese immigrants who understood both their Japanese heritage as well as American culture. A number of his instructors had been among the more than 120,000 Japanese rounded up by the American government to be sent to internment camps in Utah and other western states. But because the need for language instructors was so great, they were released to participate in this program. In essence, it was the Nisei instructors' job to prepare intelligence officers who would help defeat their ancestral homeland. Yet all of the officers were loyal to the United States and acted with complete integrity.

FIRST DUTY IN THE SOUTH PACIFIC

Bob graduated from the Navy's course, received his commission, and was sent to the South Pacific. On his very first assignment, on the island of New Caledonia, he and a Nisei companion gained extremely useful intelligence while interviewing six captured Japanese submariners. Working as a team, they developed methods to get the Japanese to open up.

While any method of indoctrination no doubt strengthened the suicidal resolve of most Japanese troops, it backfired to the advantage of American interrogators when dealing with captured Japanese military prisoners. Bob and his companion could point out logically that as surviving prisoners they now had nothing to lose by cooperating and providing "normal, routine information." Unexpectedly decent treatment from Americans often prompted the Japanese prisoners to question Japan's official propaganda and the doctrine of mandatory suicide.[4]

In this case, the six prisoners on New Caledonia gradually gave crucial information regarding extremely long-range submarines (14,000 miles) that had reached the west coast of the United States to attack an oil refinery and to sink ships departing to Hawaii and other military destinations. They even revealed that these submarines carried small float planes that allowed them to communicate quickly, and without radio, with other boats in the vicinity. This information proved of great value to naval command in forming strategies to thwart enemy technology. Bob Sheeks's naval service was off to a great start.

SAVING ENEMY LIVES ON SAIPAN AND TINIAN

It was in preparation for the invasion of Saipan, northeast of the Philippines, that Bob found his true calling in the war. His experience in New Caledonia proved the value of interrogating Japanese prisoners with respect. But they had to acquire prisoners, which was the first challenge. Their strict cultural indoctrination made it almost impossible to persuade any Japanese soldier or civilian to give up. Having thought about it a great deal, Bob approached his superior officers with two ideas.

First, they could drop pamphlets on known Japanese positions well in advance of combat. Written in Japanese, these pamphlets would offer the promise of water, food, and good treatment to both civilians and soldiers. The leaflets would be called a "Come Out Pass" to make it look normal for someone to turn themselves over to the Americans.

Second, Bob proposed the use of handheld megaphones and Jeep-mounted loudspeakers to call out to the Japanese when they were discovered. He would reinforce the offer of good treatment, as well as explain that it was honorable to save one's own life.

He realized that many would not accept the offer, but each one who did surrender would be a life saved from useless destruction. He pointed out to his commanders that American lives would also be saved because American troops would not have to approach dangerous positions to kill the Japanese.

There were a lot of intrinsic problems with his ideas. First was figuring out how to drop the leaflets from a low enough flight path that they weren't torn apart in the wind, while not exposing the pilot to unnecessary risk of being shot down by ground fire. Second, the Marines had been trained to take out the enemy—whenever and wherever possible. Getting them to hold back while Bob tried to talk the Japanese out of the caves was viewed by many as an encumbrance to progress. Plus, some suicidal Japanese had already pretended to surrender, only to blow themselves up when they reached American lines. Quite simply, the Marines didn't trust them.

In spite of this resistance, Bob received permission to outfit a special Jeep with a portable gas generator to power a strong amplifier and loudspeaker array. He also drafted three leaflets in Japanese that included the invitation to surrender, along with instructions on how to do so, such as waving a white cloth with hands above the head.

Someone in his group suggested a "patrol card" leaflet to be handed to the Marines before going on patrol in order to convince them that it was worth taking the time to allow the Japanese to surrender. The card emphasized that every prisoner taken was a way to save American lives, as well as time and ammunition. It also provided a list of Japanese phrases a Marine would need to know to supervise prisoners until they returned to base.

Many of Bob's fellow Japanese language interpreters were excited to try his approach to coaxing out the enemy. In addition to saving lives, it increased the chance of getting good intelligence from those who surrendered. Important to note is that while everyone was interested in saving American lives, Sheeks and his comrades felt that it was about saving lives, period.[5] Because there was no budget for printing, he went to the *Honolulu Advertiser* newspaper, which agreed to print thousands of copies of the leaflets at no charge.

Sheeks got his first chance to try out his new strategy in June 1944 on the island of Saipan. A group of Japanese civilians was reported hiding near the Second Marine Division. To reach them, Sheeks had to crawl up a rocky hill, carrying his megaphone and battery pack. He did his best to keep a low profile in case a Japanese sniper was in the area. Once he reached a secure spot within hearing distance, he switched on his megaphone and began to call out to the empty hillside, encouraging anyone hiding to come out to safety. He used a calm voice and made the promise that it was safe, that there was food and water available, and that other Japanese civilians were already in a camp. He assured listeners that these civilians were treated well.

Of all the promises he made, water was the most alluring. Despite the tropical climate, it was difficult to find fresh water on the island—the fugitives were likely very thirsty. Bob's first attempt proved fruitless, so he tried again. Still nothing. Then, just as he concluded that the reports of hidden civilians were in error, he saw some movement. Soon a man, a woman, and two children emerged into view. As they stumbled their way forward, Bob kept talking to them in reassuring tones until he was finally able to step out and hand them a canteen of water. The woman grasped the canteen and took a quick, desperate gulp. She paused, perhaps to see if the water was safe, and then handed it to her children, who also took deep draughts of water.

The woman told Sheeks that Japanese soldiers had told them that the Americans would kill everyone on the island. She was relieved to find that wasn't true and that he was kind to her. Sheeks accompanied the family in the back of a truck down to the camp that had been set up for survivors. He was elated to turn them over, knowing that he had saved their lives and that his idea had actually worked.[6]

Sheeks's first chance to use the loudspeaker array on his Jeep came a few days later when he was summoned to a remote hillside. The Marines were aware of a group of Japanese hiding in a cave up a ravine, and they were not eager to risk their lives crawling up the hill to throw explosives into the cave. They decided to give the language officer a chance.

The first thing Sheeks did was to instruct the Marines to put their rifles over their shoulders, rather than carry them pointing up the hill. It would be difficult to talk anyone into surrendering in the face of weapons. Then he turned on his amplifier and waited while the vacuum tubes warmed up. Finally, he started talking into the microphone, his voice amplified loud enough to be heard by anyone in the area. He spoke in even-toned Japanese, repeating the message of his first encounter—safety, water, food, shelter, and honor. The honor part was the hardest sale to make, so he repeated it with variations that included the fact that other people had come forward and were being treated with dignity and respect. He repeated his appeals until it was obvious that no one was coming out. Saddened, he prepared to leave. But just before turning off the gasoline generator that powered his amplifier, he spoke into the microphone one last time to say a polite "Sayonara" (translated, it means a very poignant "Good-bye," but with the additional meaning "if it must be so").

To Bob's surprise, faces started to emerge from the underbrush, first women and children, and then a number of men. The group was bedraggled and thirsty. When Bob shared his canteen with the desperate people a number of Marines stepped forward and offered theirs as well. Another group had been saved.

As they were preparing to get onto a truck, one of the men stepped forward and pulled a crumpled piece of paper from his shirt pocket. He handed it to Bob. It was one of the surrender leaflets. The man explained that the Japanese soldiers shot anyone who was seen with a leaflet, so he had hidden it in his clothing. Several other men who surrendered in the next few days also produced well-hidden leaflets, which suggested that the warning had helped prepare them to surrender.[7]

It didn't always turn out well. Once, as he approached a spot where a Marine said a man was hiding, Bob used his megaphone to call to the fellow from perhaps fifty yards away. Bob encouraged him to come out. To his horror, there was an explosion, and a body came flying through the air. The Japanese soldier had committed suicide rather than surrender.[8]

Bob Sheeks was brave. Not only did he travel on landing craft with the first troops to arrive on an enemy beach (which action had a very high casualty rate), but he often put his life in danger while trying to negotiate a surrender. His courage was never better displayed than when he saw a Japanese soldier in the distance taking cover behind some large rocks. Because Bob had been speaking over his loudspeakers, the Japanese soldier motioned for him to come forward. The Marine lieutenant in charge of the sector thought Bob was crazy to go out there because it could so easily be a trap. But Bob decided it was worth a try, so he moved closer. Finally, the Japanese shouted that a group of soldiers was willing to come out, but they were afraid the Americans would shoot them. Bob stood up, took off his helmet, unslung his carbine from his shoulder, and placed it, along with his sidearm, on the ground. Completely defenseless, he started walking towards the Japanese position. Here is what happened next:

> He had become familiar enough with Japanese traditions to know he should try to encourage the soldier to surrender with dignity and thus save face, a key element of their culture. But he also had no way of knowing whether all the Japanese in the cave felt the same way. It was just as likely that one of the soldiers farther back and out of sight would shoot anyway. . . .
>
> Bob was about twenty feet away, and he could see the Japanese soldier peering from behind a large boulder. Talking directly to him in soothing Japanese,

Bob said he was an American Marine who had studied some Japanese, but his language skills were not very good, and he hoped he could be understood. So there he stood, in the open, unarmed, about to face a group of Japanese combat soldiers. Behind him were heavily armed Marines itching to shoot the enemy. He didn't know which group worried him more.

The Japanese soldier came forward cautiously. Behind him were about ten others, making their way in single file to where Bob waited. The first soldier who had been talking to Bob stopped and stood directly in front of him. The others formed a straight line just behind their commander. All stood at attention. Then the Japanese officer unbuckled the leather belt that held a samurai sword in its scabbard, took it in both hands, bowed, and presented it to Bob. The rest of the Japanese soldiers also bowed. Bob received the sword solemnly. He resisted the impulse to bow in return, lest the Marines behind him take it as a sign of submission. Remaining as solemn as possible in the midst of this improbable scene, he then led the group back down from the cliffs, through the remains of the sugarcane field, and past the astonished stares of the Marines.[9]

This magnificent act of bravery—and of human dignity—saved Japanese lives and perhaps the lives of Marines who would have fought with them in the absence of a surrender. It was all done in a way that allowed them to retain their honor.

ENFORCING THE GOLDEN RULE

Bob displayed many other acts of courage. One that stands out for its humanity was when he came across a Marine officer who was berating a group of captured Japanese citizens. When the officer kicked one of the Japanese from behind, Bob raised his sidearm and pointed it directly at the officer, telling him to stop his degrading actions at once. The man was stunned to face the pistol of a fellow Marine and said that he could have Sheeks court martialed for such an act. Plus, the other Marines in the officer's unit could have intervened to shoot Bob. But rather than be intimidated, Bob simply shouted, "Then do it!" The officer shrugged and allowed Bob to take control of the prisoners. Thus, Sheeks risked both his life and his honor to protect helpless people in need.[10]

A final story beautifully demonstrates the complete abandonment of Bob's childhood resentment of the Japanese and the concern he developed for them. While out on patrol one afternoon, he came upon a spot where Marines had been using jellied gasoline flame throwers to force the Japanese out of caves. A civilian woman so horribly disfigured by burns that no one could look at her lay on the side of a dusty road. Her skin was burned away over most of her body, with gaping red wounds oozing through the charred skin. When Bob forced himself to look into her face he saw that her eyeballs had been burned away, leaving her face completely unrecognizable as human. Yet somehow this poor woman was still breathing, despite the unspeakable pain.

No one else had thought to comfort her, but Bob reached into his medical kit and took out a syringe of morphine, quickly injecting it into her arm. Her body continued to convulse, so he turned to a Marine standing nearby and asked for his morphine. When the soldier hesitated, Bob yelled at him to comply. He injected the second syringe. When even that wasn't enough he asked yet another Marine for his morphine and injected the third dose. Finally, the woman's breathing eased as her pain subsided, and after a few minutes of relative peace, she passed away quietly.[11]

A DISTINGUISHED LIFE

Robert Sheeks was awarded the bronze star for his heroic service on Saipan and Tinian by John L. Sullivan, Secretary of the Navy. Sullivan awarded Sheeks this military honor because of his effective propaganda pamphlets, which "reduced hostile resistance," thereby upholding "the highest traditions of the United States Naval Service."[12]

After the war ended, Sheeks returned to Harvard, where he graduated magna cum laude in Far Eastern Studies in 1948. He married and went on to have a distinguished career in both government and business. He lived much of his life in the Far East, including Malaya, China, Taiwan, and Singapore. Towards the end of his life, he met some of the children and grandchildren of Japanese civilians and soldiers whose lives had been saved by their accepting Bob Sheeks's invitation to surrender.

Bob and his fellow interpreters in the intelligence services saved more than 15,000 "enemy" lives. We can't know how many American lives were also saved by their not having to fight those who chose to surrender. What is certain is that many lives were blessed because of Bob Sheeks's simple humanity in the midst of total war.

CHAPTER 11

BERNIE FISHER

VALOR IN VIETNAM

L ieutenant Colonel Bernard Fisher loved flying—from his first
flight in a small crop duster near Clearfield, Utah, at age thirteen
until he rose through the ranks of the United States Air Force to
command a squadron at Hahn Air Base in Germany. Before that
time, he had flown nearly every fighter aircraft in the Air Force ar-
senal, and in two amazing "dead stick" landings, he had saved two
famed but temperamental F-104 Starfighter jets. A dead stick landing is one in which the engine has failed, but the pilot chooses to try
to land the aircraft using only its momentum. Because a Starfighter
had an incredibly short glide path (the forward distance covered
relative to speed), the military always advised pilots to bail out and
let the jet crash. Bernie safely landed his aircraft both times, saving
the country millions of dollars.

In 1966, Bernie was serving in the Vietnam War. He flew an A1-E Skyraider, a pilot-only propeller aircraft that carried more armament than a B-17 bomber in World War II with its crew of ten. The Skyraider allowed Bernie to provide close air support to ground troops, thus playing a vital role in saving the lives of United States soldiers.

On March 9, 1966, Bernie proved his remarkable skill as a pilot by guiding other aircraft into the proper attack pattern, despite heavy cloud cover that should have made the mission impossible. It was a dazzling display of skill and daring. But it was on the next day, March 10, that Bernie put his life at risk and proved his valor by helping to save the life of a downed pilot, Jump Myers, while under heavy enemy fire. In doing so he became a national hero, even in a war that was unpopular at home. Here is Bernie's story of his two most memorable missions, told in his own words.[1]

THE SILVER STAR MISSION

At this point in the Vietnam War (1966), North Vietnamese regulars had made serious incursions into the mountainous area south of the demilitarized zone between North and South Vietnam, and the Allies were hard pressed to contain them. Most of the action was taking place approximately 150 miles north of Pleiku Air Base and 50 miles west of Da Nang, our alternate air base. It was treacherous territory to fly into, with narrow mountain valleys that stream into one another in a confusing maze. Less than thirty miles from the ocean, the valleys often filled with fog and clouds making it extremely difficult to find an entrance to the valleys where ground troops needed support. To get below the clouds and fly a strafing run, you had to come in at about fifty feet. With foothills and mountains reaching elevations of nearly 7,000 feet, any false turn could prove fatal.

The valleys also provided a remarkable advantage for the North

Vietnamese anti-aircraft batteries [large gun crews] because they could mount guns on the side of the hills to fire down on us rather than up. It's much easier for a gun crew to site their weapon to fire vertically or [down] on a target that has to follow a precise angle of approach. Compared to hostile ground-fire in the lowlands, this was murderous. Our aircraft came back with holes in the fuselage on nearly every flight.

On March 4 or 5, 1966, intelligence reported that the North Vietnamese were planning a major assault on a Special Forces position in a remote location known as the A Shau Valley. The valley is six miles long and just one mile wide. Approximately 450 of our men occupied an old French fort to guard the approaches from North Vietnam, and they'd captured some North Vietnamese scouts who were very candid in telling them what to expect in the next few days. More than 2,000 North Vietnamese regulars were moving into position near the valley to trap the special forces and were already setting up machine gun nests and anti-aircraft batteries in the foothills. Though Special Forces were the best soldiers America had, they were badly outnumbered. They had a rough time of it right from the beginning when the battle started on March 6.

On the morning of March 9 I'd just finished flying one mission and was getting set to fly another when word was received that we were to scrap it because a fight was on at A Shau, and they needed our help. I said okay and changed our flight plan. Apparently an AC-47 had been scrambled out of Da Nang to provide covering fire for the ground forces using three "Puff the Magic Dragon" mini-guns. Those guns are terrible weapons, firing 6,000 round[s] per minute (100 bullets per second), which is so fast that when they're firing, all you see is a sheet of flame tearing out from the side of the aircraft with a blue haze of smoke rising from the nozzles. Hence the nickname Puff.

The AC-47 made an initial strafing run down the "tube" at A Shau. On its next pass, its left engine was hit by the North

Vietnamese. As the pilot banked to exit the area, he lost his right engine. He somehow managed to make an emergency landing and get off a "Mayday" call for help. A rescue was ordered for the crew of the AC-47, and we were diverted to provide additional support for the infantry in the fort in place of the AC-47.

Bruce Wallace was my wingman that day as we took off from Pleiku and headed northwest. The weather was extremely poor with an expected ceiling of just 300 feet in the valley. At approximately seventy-five miles out, we hit a cloud bank that made it obvious the weather was not going to cooperate, so we slid out to the west where it wasn't quite so cloudy. As we reached the general area, I started probing the canyons to figure out where the Special Forces camp was but with no success. On my third attempt I came up out of the clouds within a few yards of the nose of a helicopter, which about scared me (and the pilot of the helicopter) to death. We recovered from the near miss, and I raised him on my radio.

"Do you know where A Shau is?"

"We just came out of there—picked up some of the dead and wounded from the AC-47."

"Can you direct me in?"

"Keep going, and you will come to a saddle in the mountains. Go over the saddle and drop down into the little valley on the other side. When you see the smoke and start getting shot at, you'll know you're in the right place."

We proceeded as directed, and when we reached the area, I checked in with the airborne command post to see what they wanted us to do.

"We're being overrun and are consolidating into the northwest mortar bunker. The fort is shaped like a triangle, with a mortar bunker at each point. You can hit anything that moves on the southern wall."

The situation was extremely desperate, because the North Vietnamese knew that if the cloud covering lifted, we'd wipe them out. They stood to lose more than 2,000 troops. So, the last thing they were going to do was waste time and effort to take prisoners. It was a life-and-death struggle.

"What do you want us to do first?"

"Take out the AC-47. The guns are still hot, and if the North Vietnamese get hold of them they'll turn them on us!"

That was a pretty dangerous request. Both Bruce and I were loaded with hard bombs, which typically required a dive bomb approach to release. Usually, when you dive bomb, you start your run at 5,000 feet above the deck and roll in at about a 45-degree dive to the ground, releasing the ordnance at 2,500 feet so you won't be hit by your own blast. Otherwise, the fragmentation can flip up and hit you.

But with a ceiling at 300 feet we'd have to skip the hard bombs in, which is an extremely difficult maneuver and you're almost sure of getting hit yourself. As the on-scene commander, I decided that Bruce was best suited to pull it off, so I told him to get the AC-47. He simply said okay and headed off down the canyon to gain some room to maneuver. When he was probably two or three miles away, he executed a 180-degree turn and came back with all the speed he could get out of the old airplane. Staying just under the cloud ceiling so he could get a clear shot, he released all six bombs simultaneously then pulled the nose almost straight up and rocketed up through the clouds and broke out on top. It was amazing flying, one of the best maneuvers I've ever seen, and he managed to get up without getting hit. The AC-47 went up in a tremendous fireball that obliterated any hopes the North Vietnamese might have had of capturing it.

By this time Air Command had brought in additional aircraft to help us keep the North Vietnamese off the Special Forces. Since Bruce and I were the ones who knew the lay of the land, it now became our responsibility to guide them in for the attack.

I had Bruce stay up top to circle the area and collect the aircraft, while I stayed underneath to fire on the North Vietnamese and direct the attack when our guys got under the ceiling. From where he was on top, Bruce could see the mountain peaks that oriented him to where the approach was, and he orbited (flew in a circle) while other aircraft fell into formation behind him. When they were ready, he'd line up an approach and take them down through the clouds. By following him, they would come down through the clouds and miss the mountain peaks. We put in quite a few airplanes in that way. Eventually, though, heavier clouds moved in, and we lost our needed reference point to bring in additional planes.

After about three and a half hours, Bruce called in that he was "bingo" (running low on fuel), so we requested permission to return to base. Just about that time, two C-123 cargo planes checked in with medical supplies and ammunition. With no knowledge of the area, they couldn't find their way in to make a drop. The command post asked if we could stay and help them. I suggested that instead of returning to Pleiku, we could fly to Da Nang, which was twenty minutes' flying time away. That would give us a few extra minutes to help the big planes find their way in.

Clouds had now obscured all approaches from above, and Bruce could not find his way in. I was still flying underneath the ceiling. When you're looking down on clouds, it's all darkness. But looking up through the clouds, you can see light spots where the clouds are thinning enough that a pilot could descend and have enough visibility to make a decent approach to the target. Eventually I found a light spot, and I checked in with Bruce:

"I think I've found a hole. Why don't you get the 123s lined up and I'll fly straight up through the hole where you can see me, then I'll twist around and head straight back down through the same spot. You follow me with the 123s in trail, and we'll get them on a good approach to the fort."

"Roger. We'll be waiting."

It worked beautifully. I shot straight up through the hole, and when I reached clear sky, I twisted into a roll at the top and headed straight back down where I'd come from. It was a lot like pushing a needle up and out of fabric and then back down to complete the stitch.

When I reached the ceiling, I leveled out on a perfect angle for the approach. Bruce and the C-123s came after me. The ceiling was so low they had to drop the supplies from fifty feet, which didn't give a parachute much room to slow the fall.

On the first pass, the bundles were released successfully. The C-123s flew down the canyon and back up into the clear, where they made a 180-degree turn and came back for the next approach. The pilots in the C-123s did a great job and landed fourteen bundles in the six or seven passes we orchestrated. When the last bundle was dropped, Bruce indicated that he was now "Bingo" for Da Nang, which meant he had to get out of there fast or he'd run out of fuel. I was in about the same condition, so I sent him off and finished getting the 123s out before requesting permission to refuel.

When I reached the Da Nang area I checked in with GCA radar (Ground Control) and they gave me a precision approach into the field at Da Nang. I looked at my fuel gauge and told them I didn't have enough fuel to run the standard square box pattern where the radar gives you the vectors for landing. "You just bring me over Da Nang, and I'll run my own pattern."

When I broke out of the clouds and into the clear, I was at about 800 feet and right over the air field. I contacted the tower for permission to land while dropping my gear and flaps for a final approach.

"You are number two in the emergency pattern."

Number two? I thought incredulously. I radioed back that I couldn't wait.

"A C-123 is on final approach with a fire onboard, and he's experienced a number of explosions in primary systems. He's number
one. You're number two."

I rolled back up and looked down to see him on final approach.
He was a little bit ahead of me, so I said, "I'll take the runway, the
taxi way, or the grass in between, but I can't go around."

I landed on the runway. That forced the C-123 pilot to land on
the taxi way, which he did without any problem. I caught up with
the pilot of the 123 later and apologized, and he was fine with what
had happened.

That was a heck of a day. Bruce and I arranged to get the airplanes fueled up, ran down to the officers' club to get a sandwich
or two, and then headed back to the flight line. Our aircraft were
fueled up and ready to go, so we headed back to Pleiku, arriving at
the base at 11:00 p.m.

We went to bed exhausted, hoping to get some sleep before our
next mission. But the situation on the battlefield was getting desperate, and at 4:00 a.m., we got an unexpected wakeup call. There was
hostile action all up and down the line, and they needed as many
planes in the air as they could muster. We headed for a briefing
at sunrise. My wingman that day, Paco Vazquez, didn't have many
missions under his belt and was fairly new at flying this type of
close support, but he was a good, thoughtful pilot who kept his wits
about him. We scrambled and headed on a vector to support the
Big Red division. Just as I was about to check in with air control at
Kontum we got a call on the emergency radio frequency.

"Take your birds to these assigned coordinates. There's a fight up
there, and they need some immediate help."

"Is that A Shau?" I asked.

"Confirmed. The camp's been overrun, but some of the men
made it through the night and are still holding on."

The biggest problem when we arrived was that pilots were

having trouble finding the camp through the clouds. The terrain was intimidating, and there was a lot of uncertainty about the location of the various peaks that weren't tall enough to poke through the cloud cover. Consequently, not a lot of support was being provided to the men on the ground because it was so hard to find the way in.

One of the pilots circling at 9,000 feet suggested that some of us should head over towards Laos to see if we could find an approach from the west. I didn't know it at the time, because he used his call sign, but it was my friend Jump Myers from Qui Nhon. As the on-scene commander, I decided to accept his advice, so we took off in that direction. Partway there I spotted a hole in the clouds in a location that seemed familiar from the previous day, so I radioed to Jump that I thought we could get into the valley that way. Jump and his wingman, Hubie King, joined Paco and me in a 180-degree turn to go back to the spot. Two other pilots, Denny Hague and Jon Lucas, checked in and joined our group. I instructed them to remain orbiting in case we needed them for backup.

The valley was too narrow to handle six aircraft at once. I checked the hole a second time to make sure we were above the valley floor and was reassured to see a plowed field down below. With that, I said, "Tally-Ho," and went down first with the other three following. We couldn't fly side-by-side because the mountains were too close.

We got down below the ceiling and had pretty good visibility. I found the landmarks I needed to orient myself to the approach and started heading in the direction of the old fort. Though it helped our visibility to have the ceiling at 800 feet, it also meant that it was easier for the big guns the enemy had mounted on the sides of the hill to fire down on us. The battlefield was like a dark nightmare: the black, acrid smoke rising up in columns from the ground merged with the cloud ceiling and mixed with ash from the multiple fires created by repeated napalm strikes. Burned-out trees and wrecked vehicles were blown haphazardly on the valley floor, and I could actually smell the cordite from the explosives.

I switched over to FM radio and flew right in on the deck, buzzing the fort while contacting one of the Special Forces guys on the ground: "I'm the A-1 that just buzzed you—what can we do to help?"

"We've been overrun. There are about 180 of us left. They've got everybody else. We're with the wounded in the corner of the north-west mortar bunker. Hit anywhere else in the camp you like."

With that, I set up an attack on the south wall of the fort. We flew about two miles down the center of the valley with the North Vietnamese firing what appeared to be .50-caliber guns (.50 calibers have a red tracer rather than the green tracers used in other small weapons). That made the approach very challenging. On our first run, Hubie King, Jump Myer's wingman, got hit in the Plexiglas canopy that encloses the cockpit, making it impossible for him to see through the smoke and wind that buffeted his face. He broke off and headed to Da Nang, the nearest airfield.

Normally, we'd first set up a run to drop bombs to reduce the danger of blowing up if we got hit, but I could see the North Vietnamese swarming towards the Special Forces so decided to do a strafing run first. I set up an attack pattern where I flew in first with four cannon firing directly in front of our forces. Paco slid over thirty feet and made a second pass, followed by Jump Myers who followed thirty feet to the right of Paco. The object was to drive the Vietnamese back from our people and into the jungle. The first pass got them moving. The second and third caught and killed many of them and drove the rest away from our men. At the end of the run we circled up and to the left to set up a repeat pattern to keep backing them towards the jungle. We must have been pretty effective because command later attributed between 300 and 500 enemy dead due to our strafing.

About the time Jump completed his second run, they hit him with something big in the engine and he started to lose power. I could see him out ahead of me because I'd already entered the pattern for another run and he was trailing fire, all the way from the engine past the tail of his aircraft. I was relieved to hear his voice in my headset, "This is Surf 41. I've been hit and hit hard."

I responded immediately, "Hobo 51—Rog, you're on fire and burning clear back past your tail!"[2]

"Surf 41—Rog, I'll have to put her down on the strip."[3]

Even though Jump had a parachute on, it wouldn't do him any good because the aircraft didn't have an ejection seat and he didn't have enough altitude for the chute to open. He pulled up a little but didn't have enough power to get very high. He reported later that he briefly thought of riding it into the jungle. While it's likely that the huge propeller on the A-1E would clear out some of the trees when it hit, the fire onboard the aircraft made it even more likely there would be an explosion when he crashed.

Jump opened the canopy to get rid of the smoke, but the fire crawled right up into the cockpit. He closed the canopy and endured the smoke.

I reminded him that he had 6,000 pounds of bombs on board that he needed to get rid of before attempting to land. He pulled the emergency release, allowing the bombs to fall without exploding. Relieved of that burden, he gained enough altitude to make a 180-degree gliding turn to line up with the runway, just 200 feet below. The loss of power made it difficult for him to maneuver to avoid coming under fire from the heavy guns the enemy had positioned east of the runway.

With all the smoke in his canopy, he couldn't see very well, so I flew alongside to tell him what was happening and when to set down. He made a clean approach, but it looked like the runway was way too short to land on. I told him to raise the gear to prevent the airplane from cart-wheeling at the end of the runway. He pulled the gear up just as he touched down and I watched it fold as he landed on his belly. The aircraft settled on the runway.

He had tried to release the extra fuel tank attached to the belly prior to landing but had failed, and it blew as soon as he touched ground. A huge billow of flame went up behind him, and the fuel made a path of fire that followed him as he skidded about 800 feet before stopping. The right wing must have caught the ground at the end of his skid because it spun him a bit, and he spilled off to the right side of the runway. The flame followed him down, caught up with him, and the A-1E exploded into a huge ball of orange fire. The explosion appeared so devastating I couldn't imagine how anyone could survive, but I circled just in case. After forty seconds with no movement I called in that he probably wasn't going to make it.[4]

Suddenly, Jump emerged from the cockpit. Just at that moment the wind picked up, and it blew the flames away to the right side of the aircraft, clearing an escape path through the smoke. He ran across the wing and dropped into the field where he raced for a muddy little ditch. Despite enemy fire, he was able to slide into the ditch for cover and covered his face and body in mud to camouflage himself as much as possible.

I contacted the command post, reported that Myers was alive, and requested a rescue helicopter. The Marines who were supporting us out of a base called Phu Bai said the chopper would be there in about twenty minutes. We returned to our strikes—both to protect Jump and provide cover for the south wall of the fort. After about ten minutes of circling and firing, I called the command post to ask them where the chopper was and they replied that it was still probably twenty minutes out. In other words, they were guessing and had no real idea how long it would take. Command asked if we'd come up out of the clouds and escort the rescue chopper back down when it arrived.

That wasn't an option. Jump's position was so precarious that if any of us pulled out, the Vietnamese would immediately swarm in and kill him. Even with our covering fire, it was down to a matter of minutes before they'd overrun his position. I considered the state of affairs on the ground to determine the feasibility of going in for a landing, but it didn't look very good. The physical condition of the runway was terrible, and it looked too short to accommodate an A1-E, anyway. I called airborne command and asked the length of the runway. They replied that it was 3,500 feet. A quick mental calculation showed that with the current wind conditions I might be able to land in 3,000 feet. Even in the best of conditions, however, it was almost suicidal to land an aircraft as large and slow as the A1-E in an area exposed to direct enemy fire. A helicopter crew can fire their weapons from the side doors to hold the enemy at bay while executing a rescue, but I'd be defenseless while sitting on the ground.

It made no sense, but I felt a strong impression that I should do this. Jump was one of the family—one of the fellows we fly with—and I couldn't stand by and let him be murdered without at least trying to rescue him. I said a quick mental prayer, asking for help, and the feeling I received seemed to confirm that I should attempt a rescue.

I reported my decision to airborne command, and they strongly discouraged it. I didn't want to go in but decided to go with my feelings in spite of their advice. I backed off and flew into the wind over the runway. Smoke coming out of the fort obscured my visibility as I dropped the gear and flaps. I entered the pattern on a good approach, but when the smoke thickened around me, I couldn't be sure—it would have been disastrous to cut the power if I wasn't over the runway. I kept the power on until I broke out of the smoke, and sure enough I was right over the runway. I cut the power and touched down.

When I hit the ground, it was obvious I couldn't stop the

airplane. The makeshift runway was constructed out of pierced steel planking that was very slick on top. To add to that problem, the North Vietnamese had hit it with mortars in a number of places, tearing the planking into jagged steel shards that I'd have to maneuver around if I didn't want to blow out my tires. All kinds of other garbage was strewn on the runway. Metal barrels and fragments of tin roofs had been blown onto the runway from all the bombing, and somebody had dropped five or six rocket pods that I hit. In spite of my dodging and weaving, I couldn't get enough of a grip to land. I powered up, bounced off the runway, decided to come in from the other direction. That was going to make for a very tough landing because I was no longer flying into the wind, which helps you slow down.

After making the turn, I touched down right at the end of the plating and immediately stood on the brakes, skidding down the runway. The brakes began to fade from heat as I reached the 2,000-foot mark, and I realized that control must have been wrong about the length of the runway (they'd actually misread the map and the runway was just 2,500 feet).

I was going to run out of runway, so I searched for the best place to go and saw some brown grass at the end that might support me. I went off the runway and over a little embankment that slowed me down a bit and slid into what turned out to be a fuel storage dump. There was a bunch of 55-gallon fuel barrels in there I couldn't avoid. Luckily, the wings passed over the top of most of the barrels, but I damaged the right wing and knocked a couple of barrels over with the tail section. Fortunately, they didn't explode. My original plan had been to set down right by Jump, but the change in landing direction put me at the opposite end of the field. I had to taxi back approximately 1,800 feet, in full view of the enemy.

Meanwhile, Paco Vazquez had lost radio contact, so he didn't realize what I was up to until after I'd landed. At first he thought I was making a crash landing as well, but when I pulled up after the first attempt and circled, he realized that I was going to try for a rescue. He, Hague, and Lucas provided covering fire by flying almost at ground level between the North Vietnamese and Jump and me. In doing so, they made themselves obvious targets for the enemy.

When I taxied past Jump, I saw him waving his hands. I hit the brakes and stopped. He ran behind the airplane and then I couldn't see him anymore. I waited for him to stick his head up over the canopy, but he didn't appear. That's when I realized I was being peppered with ground fire striking the aircraft and figured he must have been hit trying to get to the airplane. I set the brakes and went over the right side to get out and find him. When I climbed out onto the wing, I turned and saw a pair of red eyes staring desperately from the back of the wing.

Because the A1-E sometimes stalls at idling speed, I'd left the engine running fairly fast. The airflow from that big 14-foot four-bladed propeller was blowing him off the trailing edge of the wing, and he didn't have the strength to fight against it. I slid back into the left seat and brought the power down to idle, deciding it was worth the risk of a stall.

I moved back to the right seat to help him and looked out in time to see that he'd managed to find the rough coating on the wing where you're supposed to walk. He was crawling up on his hands and knees. He made it up to the cockpit and sort of straddled it, too exhausted to pull himself in. I grabbed him by his flight suit and pulled him into the cockpit head first, and he crumpled to the floor. He looked up and gave me a weak smile, mumbling something like, "You are one crazy son of a gun."

Normally, we'd have strapped in, but there was no time for that. The enemy was hitting us pretty hard with small arms fire from just thirty feet away, so I slid down into the seat, opened the throttle and away we went, hoping like the dickens that we had enough runway to get airborne. I held the aircraft on the ground until I was almost at the end of the runway and then pulled and rotated. It came off the ground okay, and we streaked up into the safety of the sky, breaking out of the clouds at about 11,000 feet.

When we made it up and off the runway, Paco moved in next to my wing. I brought the aircraft onto a level flight path and then debated with myself whether to go to Da Nang or Pleiku. Pleiku had a better hospital, but the aircraft had been pretty badly hit, and I didn't know if I'd have mechanical trouble. Everything seemed to be operating okay, so I told Jump that if he felt okay, we'd head to Pleiku.

"Whatever you want to do."

I headed for Pleiku, although I remember thinking, *If it quits on the way, I'll wish like the devil I'd gone to Da Nang.*

I had a couple of canteens of water, which I gave him. He asked for a cigarette, but I said, "Sorry, I don't smoke." He looked terrible. He'd tried to camouflage himself by covering his face and hands with mud from the creek, which was foul with oil. It looked like he was burned all over his body from the fiery crash landing, and his clothes were covered in soot from the flames. He smelled awful, but at least he was alive.

When I got to Pleiku I thought, *Forget a pattern. I am going to land straight on the runway.* The moment we touched down, I stopped on the runway as an ambulance raced out to meet us. Two medics jumped up on the wing to help Jump out of the cockpit and into the ambulance, but he refused to get out of the airplane. No matter what they said, he just wouldn't move. I don't know why, but Jump was adamant. The medics looked him over and said they thought he was okay for a few more minutes and gave me permission to continue to taxi onto the ramp where Jump could get out on his own. I shut the engines down at the chalk line, and they headed for the hospital.

It turned out that Jump wasn't burned as badly as I had origi-nally believed, which was amazing, considering that his aircraft had started burning while still in the air and his belly tank had exploded on impact. It was a miracle, but he had survived, and we'd made it back to the safety of our airbase.

THE MEDAL OF HONOR

As the story of Bernie's daring rescue circulated in the camps around Vietnam, the press corps immediately began to ask ques-tions about it. That Bernie had flown a fixed-wing aircraft (instead of a helicopter) to rescue a man on the ground while under intense enemy fire was virtually unheard of. As one of his support team said, "The thought of doing it had simply never crossed our minds."

The reason helicopters are used for such rescues is that they can come down quickly with gunners providing covering fire while the rescue is in effect and then rise directly from the spot to safety. But a fixed-wing aircraft is fully exposed during the landing time on the ground and on the take-off run. The chance of a pilot being killed is so high that it can't be calculated. But Bernie had a man on the ground, and he felt he had to do his best to save him. He did this knowing that he himself had a wife and five children at home in the United States, which meant that he risked everything he had. But such was his devotion to the men under his command that he went in, regardless of the risk. In doing so he provided service "above and beyond the call of duty" and showed "valor" in combat (*valor* is the word that appears on the Air Force Medal of Honor that he received).

His commanders on the ground, who verified the details of his mission, recommended Bernie for the Medal of Honor. This award, the highest honor bestowed by the United States on an active duty soldier, was authorized by Congress and presented by President Lyndon B. Johnson. In receiving this honor, Bernie became a lifetime ambassador for the United States Air Force. His life was worthy of the distinctions he earned. Bernie passed away on August 16, 2014, in Kuna, Idaho. He was a dedicated warrior but a gentle and thoughtful man. His name will be honored as long as there is a United States of America.

CHAPTER 12

KIM PHUC

FIRE IS FALLING FROM HEAVEN

Napalm is essentially jellied gasoline—a highly flammable gel that sticks to a person's skin while burning at temperatures in excess of 1,800 degrees Fahrenheit. Almost certain death results if more than 15 percent of a person's body is burned. Though used somewhat in both World War II and the Korean War, napalm became synonymous with the Vietnam War. The United States and its South Vietnamese allies dropped more than 340,000 tons of this incendiary during the course of the war. Its primary use at the outset was to destroy buildings, bridges, and infrastructure. But over time it became an antipersonnel weapon to hurt, kill, and demoralize the enemy. The few who survived a napalm attack have lived with pain and scarring for the rest of their lives.

None of this was evident to the American public in 1972. Even though television brought images of the war into American homes every night on the news, to most it was a far-off conflict that held little meaning except to those who were there. Unlike previous wars, in which the intentions of both sides were clear, the objectives of the Vietnam War were ambiguous. Three years earlier, a massacre by American forces of more than five hundred Vietnamese civilians, including women and children, at the village of My Lai had shocked American sensibilities. It called into question American motives for being there, as well as the burdens the war inflicted on our soldiers. Yet, while anti-war protests flourished, most Americans still supported President Richard Nixon in his promise to implement a "secret plan" for ending the war (a phrase he used to get elected). The country was divided along ideological lines, some saying, "My country, right or wrong," and others shouting, "Hell no, we won't go." By 1972 the war had been going twice as long as World War II with no territory gained, the enemy apparently undiminished, and nearly 50,000 Americans dead.

What was not clear to most Americans was the suffering of individual Vietnamese citizens who lived in constant chaos and uncertainty. But America's lack of awareness changed in an instant on the morning of June 9, 1972, when a single photograph published on the front page of the *New York Times* and in other newspapers around the world made clear the unbearable suffering inflicted by war.

The photo is remarkable, even today. It was an almost impossible shot to take, but Nick Ut happened to be standing directly in the path of children running from a napalm attack gone awry. The image of agony and terror on the faces of Vietnamese children was so searing that the public was shocked as never before. Ut's photo quickly became an iconic image of the war. Regardless of ideology, it was evident to anyone who viewed the photo that no one should ever have to experience such agony and terror, particularly a little child whose clothes were burned off her body. Nick Ut's photo helped turn the tide of public opinion against the war.[1]

As for the suffering child in the photo, she became known as "the girl in the picture." Her name was Phan Thi Kim Phuc. Kim is the family name, placed first in order in Asian societies, and Phuc (which rhymes with *look* or *hook*) is the child's individual name.

Fortunately, Phuc's life didn't end that day, even though more than 35 percent of her body was burned by napalm. The story of Phuc's journey through pain, and of the many people who reached out to help her, is inspiring. Today, she is alive and well—and a wife and mother who still lives with pain but who has found peace.

A PROSPEROUS CHILDHOOD
INTERRUPTED BY WAR

Kim Phuc was born on April 6, 1963, in the village of Trang Bang, on the main road from Saigon, in South Vietnam, to Cambodia. Years earlier her mother had turned a skill for making homemade noodle soup into a prosperous restaurant business. She served hundreds of meals a day, employing Phuc's grandmother and other family members in the process. The workday started before 2:00 A.M. to get ready for serving breakfast at 5:00 A.M. The day ended at night when the family made noodles for the following morning. It was hard work, but it enabled the Kim family to enjoy financial security that eluded most families of their class. In fact, they became wealthy and built a large family home in which young Phuc grew up.

Even though the war in Vietnam raged during her childhood, the effect on the family was indirect. No battles were fought in their neighborhood. Because their village, Trang Bang, was on the main road between Saigon (the capital of South Vietnam) and Cambodia, where many North Vietnamese soldiers infiltrated their way into South Vietnam, the village was always busy. There were four major groups in the Vietnam War:

- The North Vietnamese regulars, whose goal was to reunite all of Vietnam as a single, Communist country;
- The South Vietnamese regulars, who fought to remain free of the Communist North;
- Viet Cong, who were South Vietnamese citizens sympathetic to North Vietnam and who operated as terrorists within South Vietnam to bring down their government;
- The American military, which supported the government of South Vietnam, ostensibly to halt the spread of Communism in southeast Asia.

The war didn't affect most South Vietnamese citizens except when they were forced to choose sides. That was a potentially fatal decision, for if one backed the South, the Viet Cong might strike to set an example. If one backed the Viet Cong, the regular South Vietnamese army would take revenge.

Phuc's family had to play both sides. Viet Cong would show up at their home at night seeking food and sometimes refuge for wounded comrades. To refuse would be to invite reprisals. But during the day, the family played the role of loyal citizens of South Vietnam. While Phuc was largely unaware of this double life, it placed an incredible strain on her parents as they struggled to support their family of six children and their extended family. Had the South Vietnamese troops suspected they were aiding the Viet Cong, the restaurant would have been destroyed and Phuc's parents imprisoned.

By the spring of 1972, the Nixon administration had reduced United States troop strength in Vietnam to around one-quarter of America's peak involvement. Nixon's strategy of Vietnamization was to transfer military responsibility from U.S. forces to the South Vietnamese military, while still providing weaponry and supplies to help the South resist the North. What neither the U.S. nor South Vietnam knew was that the Communist leaders in North Vietnam

had prepared a tremendous military offensive to shatter the morale of South Vietnam and give North Vietnam greater negotiat-
ing power at the Paris Peace Talks, then under way. This assault,
launched in April 1972, was known as the Easter Offensive. It
brought the war directly to the village of Trang Bang.

A MISTAKEN TARGET

The road the Viet Cong and North Vietnamese soldiers used
to make their way from the jungles of Cambodia toward the South
Vietnamese capital at Saigon took them through Trang Bang.
Naturally, the South Vietnamese counterattacked. Though Phuc's
parents were on reasonable terms with the local Viet Cong, they
realized no one could protect them in an all-out battle. So, they
moved their family from the comfort of their large home to a small
building on the compound of the Cao Dai Temple, the most prominent landmark in Trang Bang. They hoped that the warring armies
would respect the sanctity of this religious shrine and the family
would be safe there. They were joined by several other families in the
outbuilding, including Phuc's grandmother, two aunts, and three
cousins. In the course of the next two days, they felt the concussion
of nearby bombs and the sound of gunfire outside the compound.
On one occasion, Phuc's mother attempted to leave the compound,
only to be driven back by a rocket attack. Although gunfire in the
city was sporadic, the adults felt compelled to keep the windows
and doors closed. The heat was sweltering, and people inside the
crowded building struggled for fresh air.

On the morning of June 8, 1972, the South Vietnamese commander told international journalists in the area that he had re-
frained from using air strikes against the Viet Cong because a single
strike could destroy the village, but his field commanders were
pressing for an air assault to reinforce their ground efforts. By this
point in the battle the Viet Cong had been driven from the center

of Trang Bang to the eastern edge of the village near the Cao Dai Temple. That was where the day's fighting was going to take place.

The airstrikes began with raids by American-built A-1 Sky-raiders, pilot-only single-propeller aircraft capable of carrying a large load of bombs. The attack started with bombs to blow apart buildings and reinforced bunkers. Napalm canisters soon followed to burn out enemy troops. Occasionally helicopters came in to provide close covering fire for the South Vietnamese ground units. Fortunately, even though the Viet Cong had now been reinforced by North Vietnamese regulars, both sides still respected the temple and avoided putting it into a cross fire.

But in the late afternoon a small South Vietnamese observation plane fired two white flares into the center of the temple grounds, sending up columns of white smoke, which marked the area as a North Vietnamese position. Soldiers inside the compound rushed out to set off two colored-smoke grenades, one violet and one yellow, to identify the spot as a position held by South Vietnamese forces. In other words, the signals were contradictory, and it was up to South Vietnamese and American aircraft pilots to make up their mind which of the two signals to believe. The drone of an approaching bomber quickly provided the answer, and the soldiers ordered the civilians inside the temple compound to run for their lives.

This was a second source of confusion for the approaching American pilots. Their rules of engagement stated that a running target was likely hostile, because friendly forces would stop and turn to face an approaching aircraft. But of course the frightened villagers did not know that, and so they continued running in terror as the first aircraft released its two bombs. The pilot should have turned away when he saw the colored smoke but failed to do so. Miraculously, both of his bombs malfunctioned and failed to explode. Unfortunately, a second Skyraider, following close behind the first, compounded the mistake and released his napalm canisters directly behind the running civilians.

Unlike a bomb, which follows an arc to the ground before exploding on impact, a napalm canister often tumbles in the air, giving it a forward rolling motion when it hits the ground. As the canisters crack open to release their fiery gel, they spray a broad pattern in front of where they land to disperse the flaming liquid over a wide area. For the small group of people running from the pagoda, the effect was a shower of volatile fuel splashing them from behind and raining down from above. The sky darkened with acrid smoke through which hazy images of temple spires could be seen reaching up towards heaven.

CAPTURING THE WAR IN A SINGLE PHOTO

These conditions had been experienced countless times during the Vietnam War. What made this incident unique was that a group of international journalists had lined up on the road to the temple in the hope of getting a good photo to send home to their news service that evening. None had expected to be faced with a group of civilians and soldiers racing directly towards them as their world went up in flames. But that is what they saw now. The brave ones held their ground on the road as they snapped photo after photo of people running toward them from the eerie and awful scene of people fleeing a temple disappearing behind a wall of smoke and fire.

From this unique position, Nick Ut captured the haunting portrait of nine-year-old Kim Phuc screaming in pain as she ran from the napalm that burned away her clothes and the flesh on her back. Of course, Nick and the other journalists had no way of knowing exactly what images their cameras were capturing, but they knew that this was a moment unlike any other in the history of the war.

What actually happened to Phuc and her family is even more disturbing than the photo shows. With Phuc's help, Denise Chong wrote in her book *The Girl in the Picture* about the moments just after four napalm canisters rained their flaming gel onto the fleeing family:

> There was a deafening pop. Auntie Anh's baby was thrown from her arms, and she buckled at the knees. Instinctively, she clutched at the back of her left leg. The fingers on that hand instantly fused from coming into contact with the gob of jellied napalm burning there. The soldier who had picked up Danh [Phuc's three year old cousin] took a direct hit of enough napalm that it incinerated him and left the child with devastating burns. Grandmother Tao found the blackened body that was her grandson and carried him farther . . .
>
> Phuc was struck with such force from behind that she fell face first to the ground. . . . She did not wake up to what was happening until fire enveloped her. Fear took over. She would not know that she had got to her feet, had pulled at the neck of her burning clothes—in the way one would in discomfort on a hot day—and that what was left of them fell away. Her first memory of the engulfing fires was the sight of flames licking her left arm, where there was an ugly, brownish-black gob. She tried to brush it off, only to scream out at the pain of the burn that had now spread to the inside of her other hand. In that instant, Phuc knew that she had touched burned flesh. She had taken a hit of napalm to her left side, on the upper part of her body. It incinerated her ponytail, burned her neck, almost all her back and left arm.[2]

When Phuc emerged from the flame behind a half dozen other children, she was crying out the Vietnamese phrase for "Too hot, too hot!" Christopher Wain of ITN grabbed her arm to bring her to a stop and gave her water. Nick Ut went to find something to cover her. Another journalist poured cold water on her back and arm to provide relief from the burns. Normally, that is the best treatment for a burn, but with napalm it increases the intensity of the pain, and Phuc fainted in the road.

Her father pleaded with the journalists to take his daughter to a hospital in Saigon. It was her only hope of survival. Though the journalists wanted to help her, they each wanted to get to their respective photo laboratories as quickly as possible to develop the film in their cameras. There was intense competition for the photos to make the front pages of newspapers around the world. Nick Ut, a young Vietnamese photographer, was as anxious as all the others to develop his film, but he agreed to take the girl and a badly burned woman to Saigon in his car. He felt great apprehension, both for his suffering companions and for the danger they all faced in making their way through the war zone to Saigon.

A FATHER'S LOVE

Phuc's story took an ominous turn after she disappeared into the night with Nick Ut. Her parents lost track of her in all the commotion. When the family assembled later that evening, they could account for everyone but Phuc. Her little cousin Danh had died from his burns an hour after the attack. Another baby cousin would live a month before perishing. These were the only two to die from the misguided attack at the temple.

Tung (her father) and Nu (her mother) searched frantically for their daughter. A neighbor told them that a journalist had taken Phuc to a hospital near Saigon. Phuc's mother endured a fitful night, convinced that her daughter was in a morgue, an anonymous victim of the war.

The next morning, June 9, Tung and Nu left the family to travel by foot to Saigon in search of their daughter. They asked for her at the hospital closest to their village but were told that no one with napalm burns had been admitted. In despair they spent the night on a porch. The second morning after the attack they went to Saigon's largest hospital, but she wasn't there either. They were told to go to Children's Hospital. But no girl with burns had been admitted there. They decided to search every room in the hospital, just in case. She was not there. Finally, sitting on the steps of the hospital in despair, Phuc's father asked a maintenance worker if he had seen a girl brought in, perhaps already dead. The worker pointed to a small building separate from the hospital and indicated that children were sent there to die. There her parents found Phuc, curled up in a painful ball, her flesh burned and infected. Her mother picked her up gently and rocked her. Young Phuc was barely conscious.[3]

It looked as if Phuc's fate was sealed. If she stayed in this hospital, she would perish. The only medical facility in all of South Vietnam capable of treating her wounds was the Barsky Unit at Cho Ray Hospital. But the Barsky had such a long waiting list of children who had a chance of survival that it seemed impossible they would admit this suffering girl who would almost certainly die.

Then the miracles began.

THE BARSKY UNIT AT CHO RAY

On the same day Phuc's parents arrived at Children's Hospital, a number of the photographers who were with her at Trang Bang, but didn't see her rescue, went in search of the missing girl. Finding her at the hospital, they learned she would likely die because the care she needed was not available there. They immediately went to work, calling the American embassy to secure permission for her to be admitted to the Barsky Unit, a special facility built by an American charity, Children's Medical Relief International. Its goal was to provide surgery for children disfigured in war. Named for Dr. Arthur Barsky, a pioneer in reconstructive surgery, the center provided its care at no cost to the young victims. Because donors as well as the U.S. and South Vietnamese governments covered the costs associated with the hospital, the Barsky Unit needed permission to treat Kim Phuc. The photographers at the site during the napalm explosions made the necessary calls.

Even so, when the ambulance taking the injured girl turned up at the Barsky, it was not at all certain they would admit her. After all, other children with a better chance of survival were ahead of her, and taking on a patient with so little chance of living would divert precious resources from their treatment. But when Dr. My, the admitting physician, heard Phuc crying out in pain, she involuntarily exclaimed, "She's suffering!" Then she turned to Phuc's parents and said, "We will try to help your daughter."[4] Saving her life seemed impossible, but at least now she had a chance to receive care from some of the best physicians in the world.

In the end, it took fourteen months in the hospital and seventeen surgeries, but Phuc lived.[5] So extensive were her injuries that she had the longest stay of any patient admitted to the Barsky Unit.

During that time her father, Tung, stayed at her bedside almost twenty-four hours a day. One day, in the third month of Tung's bedside vigil, he was certain he saw her attempt to open her eyes. He leaned forward. "Phuc," he whispered, "do you know your father?"

There was no reply. He asked again.

"Know," she whispered.

The next morning, Tung took a bus to Trang Bang. He went directly to the noodle shop, announcing, "Phuc has come back to herself!"[6]

LIFE AFTER THE WAR

After the war Phuc returned home but not to her house. The bombing had left it uninhabitable; it never again served as the family home. When America withdrew from the Vietnam War, the Communist North Vietnamese government seized control of all property in Vietnam, and the Kim family had to build a new life.

Phuc continued to require medical care because of the extensive damage caused by the burns over more than a third of her body.

Nick Ut, who continued to visit Phuc at the Barsky until he was evacuated before the fall of Saigon, moved to California after the war. His photo of nine-year-old Kim Phuc and her cousins on the front page of the *New York Times* and other major newspapers around the world shocked the public. Overnight, the young Vietnamese photographer became world famous. He won the Pulitzer Prize for his photo, which changed the trajectory of both his career and his life forever. Even today, American veterans of combat in the war in Vietnam approach him to express gratitude for the picture he took. Some believe his photo was the tipping point in bringing the war to an end.

Meanwhile, Phuc, by then a young adult, was studying medicine when the Communist government of Vietnam summoned her for interviews for propaganda films showing the evil consequences of America's involvement in the war. This was embarrassing to Phuc because the photograph showed her naked. But she had no choice under an authoritarian regime. She felt used and humiliated.

When an opportunity came for her to continue her studies in Communist Cuba, she jumped at the chance. There she met her future husband, Bui Huy Toan, a fellow student from Vietnam. For their honeymoon, they traveled to Moscow, Russia. On the way back to Cuba, they left their aircraft during a refueling stop in Gander, Newfoundland, Canada, and sought political asylum. It was granted, and the couple settled in a small city on the outskirts of Toronto, Canada.

Originally embarrassed by the photo that made her famous, Phuc ultimately came to view it as a way to teach people about war and the suffering it inflicts on people, including innocent children. In 1996 she traveled to Washington, D.C., where she met Ron Gibbs, a Vietnam War veteran and member of the board of the Vietnam Veterans Memorial Fund. From their conversations came the idea of creating a new foundation to help children of war. In 1997 Kim Phuc founded the Kim Foundation International—Healing the Children of War. The same year, UNESCO named her a goodwill ambassador for peace. In addition to serving on boards of other groups, she is a member of the advisory board of Free Children's Foundation in Canada, and the World Children's Center in Atlanta, Georgia. Phuc is also a recipient of the Queen's Golden Jubilee Medal and the 2004 Order of Ontario.[7]

FORGIVENESS AND FREEDOM

When Phuc went to Washington, D.C., in 1996, the Memorial Fund board invited her to attend a ceremony at the Vietnam War Memorial. There she met John Plummer, the American pilot who had coordinated the attack on her village. He felt great remorse—though his choice that day had been based on faulty information—and hoped that somehow he could meet the now-grown little girl who had been harmed by his action. Phuc saw the pain in his face when they met, and he cried out, "I'm sorry. I'm so sorry."

She replied simply, "I forgive, I forgive."[8]

Injured by the South Vietnamese and their allies and exploited by the Communist North Vietnamese, Phuc's journey to fulfillment and grace was not easy:

"My heart was full of hatred, I hated my life," Phuc said. "Every time I look at my scar, I hated it and every time I got the pain . . . I couldn't bear that. I almost give up, but then it's amazing turning point, when I prayed, 'God, please help me.'"

Phuc, who became a Christian at age nineteen, turned to her faith to heal her emotional wounds.

"Faith has helped me, give me a thankful heart," she said. "To be here in this life and to have another chance in my life, it's a miracle. I was supposed to be dead."[9]

Kim Phuc would not have survived had it not been for the kindness of strangers and the love of her family. Nick Ut risked everything to take her to a hospital for emergency care. He checked on her many times through the years and helped in every way possible to smooth her path to recovery.

Along that path was the small group of photographers who contacted the American Embassy to get her admitted to the Barsky Unit, which was partially funded by American donors who cared for children they would never meet.

Finally, she might not have recovered as quickly had it not been for the loving devotion of her father, who sat beside her hospital bed for nearly fourteen months to give her hope and encouragement. He could not have done that had it not been for the tireless work of her mother operating the noodle house to support the family.

Kim Phuc most certainly would have perished had it not been for the doctors, nurses, and attendants who patiently tended to her burns, nurturing her through numerous surgeries to repair the damage inflicted by the napalm.

THE HUMANITY CONTINUES

Forty-three years after Phuc was injured in Vietnam, she received a chance to have the continuing pain of her scars relieved through the generosity of Dr. Jill Waibel at the Miami Dermatology and Laser Institute. In 2015 Dr. Waibel started a series of laser treatments to soften the thick scar tissue that covers Phuc's arm and back. Hopefully the treatments will relieve the deep pain that has afflicted Phuc for four decades. In her usual upbeat way, she told the Associated Press reporters on her arrival in Miami, "So many years I thought I have no more scars, no more pain, only when I am in heaven. But now—heaven on earth for me!"[10]

In this article, Phuc also speaks of "Uncle Ut," the photographer who rescued her, who still works for the Associated Press at age sixty-five in Los Angeles. "He's the beginning and the end," Phuc told the AP. "He took my picture, and now he'll be here with me with this new journey, new chapter."[11] Ut has been a lifetime guardian angel to the nine-year-old girl who came crying to him in the dark days of the war.

Phuc's is a story that shows both the inhumanity of war as well as the humanity of people who reach out to help others in their time of greatest need. Phuc works now through her foundation and in her roles as a goodwill ambassador for UNESCO to help other children injured in war.

PART TWO

TRIBUTES TO COMPASSION

CHAPTER 13

HUNTER SCOTT

JUSTICE FOR CAPTAIN MCVAY
OF THE *USS INDIANAPOLIS*

Hunter Scott was twelve years old when he began demanding justice for the commander of the *USS Indianapolis,* Captain Charles Butler McVay III. McVay was in command when the *Indianapolis* was sunk by two Japanese torpedoes just a few minutes past midnight on July 30, 1945, while on their way back from a top secret mission to Tinian Island in the Pacific.

In his remarkable quest for justice, young Hunter Scott appeared on the *NBC Nightly News* and was interviewed by Tom Brokaw. He was also featured in John F. Kennedy Jr.'s *George Magazine* and in newspapers around the country. Ultimately Hunter testified before the United States Senate, asking Congress to overturn what he viewed as the unjust conviction of Captain McVay for "hazarding his ship" in the last days of World War II.

The outcome of the congressional hearings and subsequent actions by the United States Navy brought a measure of healing to the remaining survivors of the *USS Indianapolis,* whose incredible suffering had been marginalized for purposes not evident to the public when the court-martial was held in 1946. There was nothing in it for Hunter except a chance to do something right in the world. It offered a chance of peace for the survivors of the *USS Indianapolis* and for Captain McVay, who, brokenhearted, had taken his own life in 1968. None of that would have been possible were it not for the merciful actions of Hunter Scott.

A TOP SECRET MISSION

In the early summer of 1945, the *USS Indianapolis* was being repaired in San Francisco. A kamikaze attack had nearly destroyed the capital ship, one of the largest and most important warships in the fleet. With at least three weeks of repairs left before sea trials, Captain McVay received urgent orders to prepare to ship out on a top secret mission. Repair work accelerated while McVay recalled his men from all over the country for the early departure. At the last minute, a large container was loaded onto the ship and welded to the deck. No one knew what it contained, and speculation was rampant. The crew did not find out what was in the box until mid-August when news was released that an incredible new bomb had been dropped on the Japanese city of Hiroshima, killing 140,000 residents. The atomic bomb nicknamed "Little Boy" had been their secret cargo.

Shortly after leaving port, Captain McVay announced that they were on a high speed run to the island of Tinian in the South Pacific. After dropping off their mysterious cargo, the *Indianapolis* was ordered to Guam for gunnery practice before joining the fleet preparing to invade the Japanese home islands. At the time, a full-scale invasion of Japan was expected to last up to two years and cost 500,000 American casualties. The war actually ended with Japan's unconditional surrender just two weeks after the *Indianapolis* delivered its cargo to Tinian.

When Captain McVay saw on the map his assigned route to Guam, he requested a destroyer escort to protect his ship from submarine attack. Although nearly all U.S. destroyers at the time had submarine detection equipment, the much larger *Indianapolis* did not. But McVay's request was denied, his superior officer telling him there was little chance of an attack. He was also given discretion whether or not to zigzag (periodically and abruptly changing the course of the ship to make it difficult for an enemy to track it), depending on weather conditions. His superior officer did not know that there had actually been a number of sightings in the area, which should have raised alarms, but they had not been properly communicated through the command structure.

McVay was well liked as a commander. Men who served with McVay told Doug Stanton in interviews for his book *In Harm's Way*, about the sinking of the *USS Indianapolis*:

> Still, McVay tried to be his usual self, a man who liked to describe his ship as a "happy ship," and whose easygoing nature was extraordinary for a naval captain. Most commanders, enlisted men joked, were either big SOBs or little SOBs. McVay, however, was neither. He was known for his egalitarian spirit and for his graciousness. Sometimes, while anchored in a harbor, he instigated skeet-shooting sessions off the Indy's fantail. Out of nowhere, his voice would sound over the PA: "Anyone interested in fishing, join me at the bow." When new crew members came aboard, he made an effort to greet them by name, saying, "Welcome, sailor. We're going to have a happy cruise.[1]"

Before going to bed on the evening of July 29, 1945, McVay gave orders to stop zigzagging to conserve both time and fuel.

The skies were overcast; he asked to be awakened if conditions changed.

At 11:58 P.M. that night, Captain Mochitsura Hashimoto of the Japanese Imperial Navy gave the order to fire six torpedoes at the approaching *Indianapolis*. In a quirk of fate, one of McVay's deck watches spotted a dark silhouette on the horizon during a very short interlude when the moon peeked through the cloud cover. Three minutes later, two torpedoes struck. One hit the ship in a bulkhead where high-octane aviation fuel was stored for the ship's spotter plane. The tremendous explosion obliterated the bow (the front) of the ship. Momentum carried the ship forward more than a mile, even with the bow destroyed. Hundreds of tons of seawater were forced into the ship. The ship's intercom was disabled so it took a few moments for McVay to make it to the bridge to receive a damage report. McVay ordered a distress message sent out, which the radiomen did, but they could not be sure their equipment was functioning. In just minutes McVay and his officers went from damage control to abandon ship. The quickly tilting deck made it difficult for the sailors to escape, yet somehow an estimated 900 men did make it off the ship before it sank, only twelve minutes after being struck by the torpedoes. This was just the beginning of the horrors.

FIVE DAYS IN THE WATER

A series of missteps and miscues consigned an additional 600 men to perish in the water. First, although it wasn't known until much later, three ships did receive the distress signal. But all three ignored it—one because the senior signal officer had said he didn't want to be awakened, no matter what the message; another because the officer of the deck thought it was a decoy message sent by the Japanese to draw them into the line of fire; and the last because the lead signal officer was drunk.

Second, the orders given to McVay were confused about who he was to report to. Thus, no one was aware that the *Indianapolis* was delayed in reaching Guam. McVay said later that a ship at sea runs on schedule very much like a train on tracks. He was outraged that it took five days for the Navy to come looking for them.

The third problem was that several United States aircraft flew over the survivors drifting in the water, but since the pilots had no idea that a U.S. ship was missing, they didn't look down. On the fourth day, Lieutenant Chuck Gwinn, a naval aviator, happened to be looking at the ocean while securing a broken antenna on his aircraft, and he saw men in the water. At first he couldn't believe they were Americans, but closer inspection revealed the truth. He immediately radioed in their position while dropping his small amount of supplies. Had it not been for an accident to Lieutenant Gwinn's antenna, it's likely that all of Captain McVay's men would have perished.

FIVE DAYS OF AGONY

Though the waters of the western Pacific are warmer than those elsewhere, they are still ten degrees colder than a person's core body temperature. Some of the men had managed to make their way into the life rafts, but many were left in the water. They faced three mortal threats: hypothermia, salt water, and sharks. More than 200 died from shark attacks.

When asked whether he'd seen anyone attacked by the sharks, survivor Maurice Bell told Hunter Scott:

> I saw several. One man in particular comes to mind. He'd drifted off maybe fifteen or twenty feet from me, and it seemed like everything had gotten real quiet, and then he screamed as the shark attacked, and all of a sudden he went straight down, and I never saw him again. The shark must have grabbed him by the leg or something. What happened was that two or

three other sharks would see the water splashing, and then they'd come in and try to get him.[2]

The 200 men who died from shark attacks is the largest single loss of life to shark attacks in history. It was a terrifying way to die, particularly for those watching the sharks circle before closing in.

It isn't known how many perished from hypothermia or from thirst. The latter was the more painful way to die, since ingesting too much saline causes a person's lips and throat to swell shut until the person suffocates. This was a risk shared by both the men in the water and the men in the life rafts. There simply was no drinkable water other than a few drops from an occasional rainstorm.

As the days passed without food or fresh water, the men started to hallucinate. They started to see old girlfriends and islands floating on the waves with cold drinks waiting for them. Some men deluded themselves that they could swim to safety, only to drown from the exertion. Toward the middle of the fourth day, many men had the same hallucination:

> What struck Haynes [the ship's physician] as the grandest hallucination of all, however, was the moment, about midday, when the *Indianapolis* herself ghosted over the horizon and sailed back into the boys' lives. At times, they yelled that the ship was steaming toward them. At others, it was drifting peacefully below them in the clear, green water, all her flags flying smartly, her portholes relit and gleaming. Some of the boys dove down to the ship and began swimming through her long passageways, back to their bunks, to the mess halls, and to the water fountains, where they drank deeply.
>
> "I found it," they screamed in heartbreaking relief, breaking back to the surface. "There's fresh water aboard! Come on fellas, let's go! She ain't sunk!"

More boys took deep breaths and dove to the ship, and in the aqua light of their dreams they sat at tables eating ice cream and drinking tall glasses of water.

"Don't drink! Don't do it!" Haynes shouted, his throat raw, his voice breaking, as he watched their dreams turn to nightmares.[3]

By the fifth day, the men were very near the end of their endurance. But after Lieutenant Gwinn's urgent message, both ships and aircraft moved into the area to save the men who remained alive.

INJUSTICE

The sinking of the *Indianapolis* in the final days of the war gained attention that wouldn't have been possible even a month earlier, when the veil of secrecy enshrouded military operations. The press kept the sinking quiet for two weeks. Then the White House announced the ship had been sunk with heavy loss of life on the same day it announced the Japanese surrender.

The story now public, the Navy took immediate action to cover itself. Admiral Chester Nimitz in Hawaii ordered a board of inquiry, which suggested that Captain McVay had hazarded his ship by failing to zigzag or to get off an S.O.S. message. Nimitz recommended a letter of reprimand be placed in McVay's file. Instead, his senior officer, Admiral King, recommended a court-martial. People have speculated why he did that, but the most obvious reason was to cover the Navy's missteps in not providing a destroyer escort to a capital ship that did not have submarine detection equipment— and also to obscure the failures of those in command who should have noticed the ship was overdue on its expected arrival at Guam. McVay's father, a retired Navy admiral, was convinced that King ordered the court-martial to get even with him for disciplining King when he was a young ensign on a ship commanded by the older McVay. But King never said why he did it.

At any rate, against Admiral Nimitz's recommendation, the Navy convened a court-martial in Washington, D. C., and McVay was convicted. The unfairness of McVay's trial is evidenced by the fact that "the Navy had lost 436 other combatant ships during the course of the war, and none of those ships' captains had been court-martialed, even though in each case, close scrutiny might have revealed mistakes, omissions or errors in judgment that could have been avoided. Wartime was not the time to second-guess the men fighting it.[4]"

The single count on which McVay was convicted was that he should have zigzagged to make it more difficult for the Japanese to attack his ship. But that accusation was dramatically contradicted by the testimony of the Japanese captain who fired the torpedoes. The war having ended, the court flew Captain Mochitsura Hashimoto to Washington to testify against McVay. Instead, Hashimoto embarrassed the prosecution by testifying that zigzagging would have made no difference and that he would have sunk the *Indianapolis* regardless. In fact, Hashimoto said, he had hoped the ship *would* zigzag so he could get a better reading on it.

Despite the lack of precedent or compelling evidence, the court judged McVay guilty. Then all the members of the court recommended leniency because of McVay's outstanding military record, including the Silver Star and the Purple Heart. Secretary of the Navy James Forrestal remitted the sentence in its entirety and restored McVay to active duty. In other words, he was guilty but warranted no punishment. McVay was promoted to rear admiral after his retirement, an honor given in recognition of outstanding service.

HATE LETTERS TO MCVAY

The nonexistent sentence should have signaled to everyone paying attention that the court-martial was flawed from the beginning. But it was a judgment that effectively ended McVay's active military career. He was never again given command of a ship, and he spent the next three years at a desk job in Louisiana. His temperament was to let things go, and he did not fight his conviction. In fact, he found life enjoyable in Louisiana. He and his wife, Louise, started life anew when he retired after thirty years of active duty and went to work selling insurance.

Unfortunately, the conviction was misinterpreted by families of some of the men who had perished in such horrible circumstances. They believed Captain McVay had been proved negligent. For many years he received letters accusing him of murder. One shows the agony felt by one family and the venom they released on McVay. It reads, "Merry Christmas. Our family's holiday would have been a lot merrier if you hadn't killed my son!"[5]

The letters tormented him. Fortunately, he did have one reprieve when he and Louise attended the first reunion of survivors of the disaster. McVay had been nervous about attending for fear that the survivors also blamed him. He was overcome with emotion when, as he stepped down from the airplane that took him there, the men with whom he had served formed an honor guard to salute him, many with tears running down their faces.[6]

Still, the letters continued to arrive, and they continued to weigh on Admiral McVay. That aggravated the cycle of despair that had escalated when Louise died of cancer. A short time later a young grandson, whom McVay adored, also died of an illness. Though he remarried and moved to Connecticut, he became increasingly despondent. When yet another hate later arrived, he said to a friend, "I just can't take this." Not long afterward he went out on the back porch of his home, lay down on the sidewalk with his head resting on the step, and shot himself.

HUNTER SCOTT'S CRUSADE FOR JUSTICE

At age twelve Hunter Scott became interested in the story of the *USS Indianapolis* from watching the Steven Spielberg film *Jaws*.

In the movie one of the characters talks as if he was one of the men on the *Indianapolis* who witnessed the shark attacks. His curiosity aroused, Hunter started researching the story of the sinking of the *Indianapolis*. The first thing he found was that there wasn't a lot to find. This lack of information fueled Hunter's curiosity, and curiosity turned into passion. At every roadblock he encountered, Hunter became more determined to find the truth. He found ways to gain access to official records and other reports. In time he built his own library about the sinking.

After his family moved to Florida, Hunter created a science fair project about the disaster after interviewing more than 180 living survivors by telephone. He'd also studied over 800 pages of military and other documents. His display won first prize at his school but not at the regional level. He was disappointed because by now he'd become caught up in the effort by a number of survivors to get Captain McVay exonerated. None of the survivors had succeeded in their appeals to the Navy, who said the case was closed.

Fortunately, one of Hunter's family friends happened to be United States Representative Joe Scarborough, who allowed Hunter to set up his science fair display outside his congressional office in Pensacola. This led to an interview with the *Pensacola News Journal*, which was connected to the Associated Press. In one of those twists of fate, the article also appeared in Litchfield, Connecticut, where McVay had ended his life. Litchfield was also the home of Tom Brokaw of *NBC Nightly News*. Brokaw contacted Hunter to interview him on national television.

All this attention led to an invitation for Hunter to appear before Congress. There he met some of the survivors he'd interviewed by telephone. Perhaps because of the unusual situation of a teenager appearing before Congress, the press took up the story and drew attention to the cause of exonerating McVay.

In this congressional hearing Hunter revealed new information that had not been available to the original court. This included coded information that the Navy had from secretly decoded Japanese radio transmissions that a submarine was in the vicinity of the *Indianapolis*. But that information had not been shared with McVay because it was felt crucial to keep it secret from the Japanese that their code had been broken. Had McVay been warned, he would have acted differently. It was also revealed at this hearing that the *Indianapolis* had sent out a distress signal that had been received but ignored. The failure to send an S.O.S. had been a primary cause of the Navy's action against McVay at his trial.

With this additional information, as well as the fact that McVay had been singled out as the only one of hundreds of captains who experienced casualties to be court-martialed, the United States Senate sided with the men of the *Indianapolis* and their unlikely advocate, Hunter Scott. In October 2000, they passed the resolution recommended by the survivors of the sinking that Admiral McVay be exonerated. The resolution was also passed by the House of Representatives and signed by President Bill Clinton.

THE CONGRESSIONAL RESOLUTION

(A) Congress makes the following findings:

(1) Shortly after midnight on the morning of July 30, 1945, during the closing days of World War II, the United States heavy cruiser *USS Indianapolis* (CA-35) was torpedoed and sunk by the Japanese submarine I-58 in what became the worst sea disaster in the history of the United States Navy.

(2) Although approximately 900 of the ship's crew of 1,196 survived the actual sinking, only 316 of those courageous sailors survived when rescued after four and a half days adrift in the open sea, the remainder having perished from battle wounds,

drowning, predatory shark attacks, and lack of food and potable water.

(3) Rescue for the remaining 316 sailors came only when they were spotted by chance by a routine naval air patrol.

(4) After the end of World War II, the commanding officer of the *USS Indianapolis*, Captain Charles Butler McVay III who was rescued with the other survivors, was court-martialed for "suffering a vessel to be hazarded through negligence" by failing to zigzag (a naval tactic employed to help evade submarine attacks) and was convicted even though—

   (a) the choice to zigzag was left to Captain McVay's discretion in his orders: and

   (b) Mochitsura Hashimoto, the commander of the Japanese submarine that sank the *USS Indianapolis*, and Glynn R. Donaho, a United States Navy submarine commander highly decorated for his service during World War II, both testified at Captain McVay's court-martial trial that the Japanese submarine could have sunk the *USS Indianapolis* whether or not it had been zigzagging.

(5) Although not argued by Captain McVay's defense counsel in the court-martial trial, poor visibility on the night of the sinking (as attested in surviving crew members' handwritten accounts recently discovered at the National Archives) justified Captain McVay's choice not to zigzag as that choice was consistent with the applicable Navy directives in force in 1945, which stated that, "During thick weather and at night, except on very clear nights or during bright moonlight, vessels normally cease zigzagging."

(6) Before the *USS Indianapolis* sailed from Guam

on what became her final voyage, Naval officials failed to provide Captain McVay with available support that was critical to the safety of the *USS Indianapolis* and her crew by—

(a) disapproving a request by Captain McVay for a destroyer escort for the *USS Indianapolis* across the Philippine Sea as being "not necessary";

(b) not informing Captain McVay that naval intelligence sources, through signal intelligence (the Japanese code having been broken earlier in World War II), had become aware that the Japanese submarine I-58 was operating in the area of the *USS Indianapolis'* course; and

(c) not informing Captain McVay of the sinking of the destroyer escort *USS Underhill* by a Japanese submarine within range of the course of the *USS Indianapolis* four days before the *USS Indianapolis* departed Guam for the Philippine Islands.

(7) Captain McVay's court-martial initially was opposed by his immediate command superiors, Fleet Admiral Chester Nimitz (CINCPAC) and Vice Admiral Raymond Spruance of the 5th Fleet, for whom the *USS Indianapolis* had served as flagship, but, despite their recommendations, Secretary of the Navy James Forrestal ordered the court-martial, largely on the basis of the recommendation of Admiral Ernest King, Chief of Naval Operations.

(8) There is no explanation on the public record for the overruling by Secretary Forrestal of the recommendations made by Admirals Nimitz and Spruance.

(9) Captain McVay was the only commander of a United States Navy vessel lost in combat to enemy action during World War II who was subjected to a court-martial trial for such a loss, even though

several hundred United States Navy ships were lost in combat to enemy action during World War II.

(10) The survivors of the *USS Indianapolis* overwhelmingly conclude that Captain McVay was not at fault in the loss of the *USS Indianapolis* and have dedicated their lives to vindicating their Captain McVay.

(11) Although promoted to the grade of rear admiral in accordance with then-applicable law upon retirement from the Navy in 1949, Captain McVay never recovered from the stigma of his post-war court-martial and in 1968, tragically, took his own life.

(12) Charles Butler McVay III—

(a) was a graduate of the United States Naval Academy;

(b) was an exemplary career naval officer with an outstanding record (including participation in the amphibious invasions of North Africa, the assault on Iwo Jima, and the assault on Okinawa where the *USS Indianapolis* under his command suffered a fierce kamikaze attack);

(c) was a recipient of the Silver Star earned for courage under fire during the Solomon Islands campaign; and

(d) with the crew of the *USS Indianapolis*, had so thoroughly demonstrated proficiency in naval warfare that the Navy entrusted him and the crew of the *USS Indianapolis* with transporting to the Pacific theater components necessary for assembling the atomic bombs that were exploded over Hiroshima and Nagasaki to end the war with Japan (delivery of such components to the island of Tinian having been accomplished on July 25, 1945).

(B) Sense of Congress Concerning Charles Butler McVay III—With respect to the sinking of the *USS Indianapolis* (CA-35) on July 30, 1945, and the subsequent court-martial conviction of the ship's commanding officer, Captain Charles Butler McVay III, arising from that sinking, it is the sense of Congress—

(1) in light of the remission by the Secretary of Navy of the sentence of the court-martial and the restoration of Captain McVay to active duty by the Chief of Naval Operations, Fleet Admiral Chester Nimitz, that the American people should now recognize Captain McVay's lack of culpability for the tragic loss of the *USS Indianapolis* and the lives of the men who died as a result of the sinking of that vessel; and

(2) in light of the fact that certain exculpatory information was not available to the court-martial board and that Captain McVay's conviction resulted therefrom, that Captain McVay's military record should now reflect that he is exonerated for the loss of the *USS Indianapolis* and so many of her crew.

(C) Unit Citation for Final Crew of the *USS Indianapolis*—Congress strongly encourages the Secretary of the Navy to award a Navy Unit Commendation to the *USS Indianapolis* (CA-35) and her final crew.[7]

JUSTICE DELAYED

Members of Congress insisted that this resolution be inserted in McVay's official record. Still the Navy refused to set aside the findings of the original court-martial. Then nine months later and two weeks after the death of McVay's younger son, Kimo Wilder McVay, who had spent much of his adult life seeking justice for his father, the Navy publicly exonerated Admiral McVay. Secretary of the Navy Gordon R. England placed a document in his file fully exonerating him and ordered his official record purged of all wrongdoing. At the same time, the Secretary awarded the *Indianapolis* the Navy Unit Commendation. Justice was finally achieved.

The news was received with excitement by the remaining survivors of the disaster, as reported by Janis Magin in an article in the *Argus Press* of Honolulu:

> "I was overjoyed," Indianapolis survivor Giles McCoy said Thursday. "I tell you, I've been working on trying to get him exonerated since 1964. He was not guilty of anything except the fortune or misfortune of war."
>
> McCoy, 76, of Palm Coast, Florida said he first broached the idea of an exoneration to McVay at the survivor's first reunion in Indianapolis in 1960 but the captain told him not to pursue it. McVay gave the go-ahead four years later but said he doubted the Navy would agree.[8]

Ms. Magin also reported that McVay's son Kimo McVay had tried for years to achieve this outcome but had died two weeks earlier. At least he had comfort from the resolution of Congress signed by President Clinton. Despite his battle with the Navy to reverse its flawed decision, Hunter Scott joined the Navy ROTC at the University of North Carolina and served on active duty as a naval aviator after his graduation.

WHAT DOES IT MATTER?

Some may wonder why, so many years after Captain McVay ended his life, it matters if his record was cleared. There are a number of answers.

First, it was the right thing to do. A man was held responsible for the deaths of 900 men when those deaths were simply the result of the operation of war. He was a victim of the attack as well as all his crew.

Second, it mattered a great deal to the survivors of the *Indianapolis* who appreciated their captain's leadership and who felt insulted by his conviction. Saying that it was the responsibility of the *Indianapolis* to have prevented the sinking left a cloud over all the men who served on the ship. The reality was that the ship was sunk by a Japanese submarine that was doing its duty. If anything, blame rested on the failure of the Navy to keep track of one of its largest warships at sea.

Third, it makes a difference to the family members of the men who perished in the sinking and those who spent days in the water. Perhaps a corrected judgment will allow them to finally release their anger and let their loved one rest in peace.

Finally, it matters that a young man like Hunter Scott stepped forward to act against injustice, even though it did not touch him directly. Because of his age and precocious interest, he was able to gain traction in Congress where others had failed. He did something noble; he showed mercy, which led to mercy at the highest levels of government and the military. That is no small accomplishment.

CHAPTER 14

SHAWN MCKINNON
BROTHERLY LOVE IN IRAQ

United States Marine Shawn McKinnon served three tours of duty in Iraq. Unlike World War I and World War II, in which four years of all-out war brought resolution on the battlefield, the war in Iraq is one of the longest military engagements in United States history. In this modern kind of warfare, the enemy often wears civilian clothing and blends in with crowds on the street. It is a challenge to know who is friend and who is foe. Americans, who are outsiders to the country and culture of Iraq, stand out as easy targets. It is no wonder that American fighting men and women feel suspicious and fearful in such circumstances, not knowing who they can trust.

Yet for the mission of assisting the Iraqi nation to find its way to democracy, it is essential to establish trust between the indigenous people and the American troops who are there to help them.

Making that happen requires a careful balance of the heart—warily decisive when a threat manifests itself but patient enough for relationships to develop.

Although Shawn was just one of thousands who successfully navigated this minefield of vulnerability and trust, his story shows how brotherhood can grow across seemingly insurmountable cultural barriers. In the end, Shawn learned to step back from suspicion to a place where he came to care deeply for the men of the local police force among whom his unit was embedded. On his final tour and with the help of his younger brother's Eagle Scout project, Shawn extended mercy to children who have suffered as a result of war. In a place and time where hatred is strong, Shawn and his comrades found brotherly love. They became the antidote to the poison of hatred.

Shawn's story is greater than just his. It showcases the way in which the United States military has adapted to the challenges of war in places where our forces remain for years to maintain the peace. It is a paradox in which combat and humanitarian relief go hand in hand to win a righteous victory.

DE-HUMANIZING AN ENEMY

One of the most difficult tasks of the military is to convince soldiers that it is acceptable to kill people. The biblical commandment "Thou shall not kill" is almost universal in human society, taught to children as soon as they can recognize right and wrong. Yet people are forced to take lives every single day, whether in the military, in police work, or in domestic defense. To do so requires a change in one's emotional orientation such that careful, discriminate killing becomes morally acceptable.

For example, to bring respectable young men, like the Marines in the South Pacific in World War II, to the point that they did not shy away from using jellied gasoline flamethrowers to inflict incredible agony on their enemy required serious mental compartmentalization. A person has to divide people into groups—those who continue to be worthy of respect and those who do not. A soldier who kills one of his comrades continues to suffer the odium and censure of his fellows (as well as legal consequences), whereas doing the same thing to an enemy is praiseworthy.

How exactly does that bifurcation, that separation of one group from another, happen? One way is to rename the group you oppose. By simply changing their label, it is easier to think of them as an enemy, a member of a group that is out to hurt your people. Once the enemy carries this new label, it's easier to fight them without feeling remorse. This change in attitude is particularly true after someone in your group, such as a close friend, gets hurt. In the movie *Patton*, General Patton's character tells raw recruits how their conscience will allow them to kill their enemies just as soon as one of their fellow soldiers gets killed.

It is particularly troublesome for soldiers to maintain a balance between violence and compassion when the line between civilians and enemy combatants becomes blurred. In traditional wars, the soldiers on each side wore uniforms. But in such modern wars as Vietnam, Korea, and the Middle East, the enemy seldom wears a military uniform. He or she dresses like a civilian and moves through crowds of noncombatants. The result is that soldiers never know who will hurt them. This creates incredible anxiety that sometimes leads to tragic consequences.

A second way to permit violence against another person is to dehumanize the enemy. Here are some examples:

- Propaganda posters from World War I and World War II show how nations dehumanize the enemy. For example, one World War I-era Allied poster shows a large angry ape holding a terrified woman in its long hairy arms. The ape wears a German army helmet on its head, its near-human face contorted by evil. The words "Destroy This Mad Brute" were printed in bold letters, followed by "Enlist in the Army." A German propaganda poster from the same era shows Great Britain as a giant tarantula spreading its hairy legs over all of Europe. Depicting the foe as animals or insects is an obvious way of dehumanizing the enemy. These are just two examples of hundreds of such images.

- Names such as "Jap," "Kraut," and "Bosch" were used in World War II to create hostility toward the enemy— another example of labeling.

- Lurid movies were produced on both sides of World War II depicting the enemy as cruel and barbaric. They almost always involved out-of-control soldiers hurting and killing innocent bystanders.

- American slave owners dehumanized African slaves by portraying them as simple creatures incapable of making reasoned judgments and therefore dependent on their masters to maintain their lives. Shortly before the Civil War, slaveholders insisted that it was a kindness to maintain slavery rather than throw people into the uncaring world of the industrialized north. All of that ignored the fact that slave owners in the real world separated families by selling children, administering beatings, and preventing men and women from marrying. To maintain their way of life, slave-owners kept an entire race of people at a perpetual disadvantage—socially, legally, and physically.

- German society demonized Jewish people before World War II. Rudi Wobbe, a young man from Hamburg, gave a chilling example of how the Nazis dehumanized the Jews. He said that when a Jewish family was arrested in his neighborhood (for nothing more than being Jewish), the authorities invited neighbors into their home to take their goods, furniture, and clothing. The Nazis realized that once a person had taken from someone without fair compensation, their conscience would not allow them to maintain the same attitude to their former neighbors. To salve their guilt, those who took the items inevitably demonized the victims with phrases such as "who do they think they are?" and "to have such expensive things, they must have taken advantage of people." Thus, the neighbors rationalized away the unfair arrest of the Jewish family and made no trouble for the authorities.

• In our day, religious differences divide believer from unbeliever, and racial and sexual slurs are used to justify violence against people in another group.

These examples are just a small sampling of the hundreds of ways that men and women are desensitized to pain and suffering so they can act in ways that otherwise would violate their conscience.

In the end, fear is the primary reason that propaganda succeeds. By creating a group identity and showing how another group is out to hurt the original group, people set aside their moral inhabitations to serve the cause of their group.

With all that in mind, it is easy to see why acts of humanity in war are an exception. It requires individuals to rehumanize their enemies and to view them as persons who deserve their respect.

America's decades of involvement in Iraq demonstrate both sides of the dehumanization and the rehumanization story. Fortunately, when the United States moved from the role of liberator to the role of protector, the process of rehumanizing the American people in the minds of frightened Iraqi civilians began. This shift is demonstrated in the experiences of one young United States Marine.

THREE DEPLOYMENTS TO IRAQ

Shawn McKinnon enlisted in the United States Marine Corps in 2003 at the age of twenty. His service began just a few months after the United States Congress authorized the use of military force against Iraq on October 16, 2002.[1] Many reasons were offered for renewed action against the nation of Iraq, ten years after Operation Desert Storm concluded in 1991. The primary reason was the attack on the Twin Towers in New York City on September 11, 2001. Iraq was sheltering members of al-Qaeda, the group responsible for the attacks on the Twin Towers. A partial list of additional reasons for new action was summarized in a White House press release:

- Iraq's noncompliance with the conditions of the 1991 ceasefire agreement.
- Iraq's "continuing to possess and develop a significant chemical and biological weapons capability" and "actively seeking a nuclear weapons capacity" posed a "threat to the national security of the United States and international peace and security in the Persian Gulf region."
- Iraq's "brutal repression of its civilian population."
- Iraq's "capability and willingness to use weapons of mass destruction against other nations and its own people."
- Iraq's hostility towards the United States as demonstrated by the 1993 assassination attempt on former President George H. W. Bush and firing on coalition aircraft enforcing the no-fly zones after the 1991 Gulf War.
- "Iraq's continuing to aid and harbor other international terrorist organizations," including anti-United States terrorist organizations.[2]

The military action in Iraq that began on March 19, 2003, was named Operation Iraqi Freedom. The United Nations fought this second Gulf war on humanitarian, military, and antiterrorist grounds. The most immediate result of the war was the killing of Saddam Hussein, Iraq's ruthless dictator. The military action lasted less than a month.

When Shawn was first deployed to Iraq a year later, American forces were maintaining order as the United States prepared to transfer power to a new Iraqi-led government on June 28. By that time, most Iraqis saw the American military as occupiers rather than peacekeepers or liberators. This attitude represented a profound change from the year before when statues of Saddam Hussein were being pulled down in joyous celebrations in which regular Iraqi citizens hugged American troops. In the year that intervened, bitter partisan disputes between various ethnic minorities, which had been held in check under the iron-fisted rule of Hussein, tore at the fabric of the nation. Ordinary citizens felt frightened and angry by the political chaos that swept through their country, and many blamed the Americans for causing it.

Shawn was plunged into this highly charged atmosphere when he began his military service. The Iraqi people were angry and suspicious of Americans. Serving in the infantry meant that Shawn and his unit moved around the country in lightly armored Humvee motorized carriers that were highly susceptible to damage by IEDs (improvised explosive devices). It also meant that once at a location, they left even the light protection of the Humvee to meet the enemy directly in person-to-person combat. That was in 2004.

Conditions were a little different when he returned for a second deployment in 2006, and they were much different in 2009. During that five-year period, he saw a marked change in the way Iraqis viewed Americans. In Shawn's experience, feelings moderated to the point that many of the Iraqis he worked with became his friends. At least one reason for this softening was an implementation of a program to embed American peacekeepers in the lives and families of the Iraqis with whom they served. Because of a unique project carried out by Shawn and his younger brother Cameron back in the United States, he had the chance to win over even more Iraqi citizens in the areas where he served.

FIRST DEPLOYMENT—2004

Shawn described Iraq as an undeveloped country—in his words, "they didn't have much of anything at all."[3] In the areas where he served, most of the families were subsistence farmers who grew their own food and raised their own animals to eat. Iraq has an arid, desert environment, where water is precious: "very hot, very dry, dusty, sandy, and relatively flat." The water used for farming is drawn from the Euphrates River using homemade pump systems that use electricity to move water from the river to individual farms. Shawn says the Iraqi people are "crafty and clever" in their ability to eke out a living from such a difficult environment.

His first deployment was combat oriented, mostly spent fighting with foreign nationals associated with al-Qaeda, who came into Iraq from the countries of Syria, Jordan, and other surrounding nations. These foreign terrorists came specifically to kill Americans, so the situation was always tense and dangerous for U.S. Marines—particularly since it was extremely difficult to tell al-Qaeda insurgents from the native Iraqis. That meant almost anyone could be out to harm an American. Consequently, our troops kept apart from the locals as much as possible.

Adding to the tension was that these foreign combatants occasionally hired Iraqis to join in the fight by planting roadside bombs, firing machine guns, and more. The Iraqis had nothing, so a few extra dollars here or there to plant a roadside bomb gave them a low-risk way to earn some extra money for their families.

Also, the Iraqis were afraid of the Americans, perceiving them as the enemy. They tried to stay out of the way whenever a Marine convoy approached. Their fears were, in fact, justified—not by actions of the Marines but because of reprisals by insurgents. Locals found associating with Americans would be punished later by Iraqi and foreign insurgents.

Towards the end of this first deployment, Shawn and his unit were told to pack for one or two days of fighting insurgents near Haditha. The mission lasted twelve days, requiring them to live out of their Humvees and any buildings they occupied. Without adequate food and supplies, it was an especially harrowing experience.

Shawn summarized his first deployment this way: "The American presence was very disruptive—we were viewed as foreigners driving around their cities with machine guns. So the locals were not at all friendly to us, or inclined to support us." It was a hostile and dangerous situation for young men to be in with only fellow soldiers as friends.

SECOND DEPLOYMENT—2006

Attitudes toward the American Marines changed in the two years from 2004 to 2006. "There was a lot more interaction with the locals," Shawn said, "particularly with the kids. They loved us!" The Marines could now walk among the locals and often passed out candy, clothes, and soccer balls to the children. "The kids knew that if they saw an American patrol, they were going to get a handout— kind of like candy being thrown to the crowds at a Fourth of July parade back in America."

"We also saw more interaction with adult men. I was a member of my company commander's security detachment, which meant I was often deployed to meet with leaders of the local tribes to discuss their needs. We talked about how to rebuild their infrastructure, including schools and police departments. Occasionally we ate a formal meal with them. They were very businesslike." Shawn said that he and his fellow Marines were still hesitant when approaching a group of locals because the enemy didn't wear uniforms. Despite this anxiety, they had to put themselves out in the community, exercising trust, because that was the only way they could help rebuild the infrastructure destroyed in combat.

The only group that did not interact with the Marines in

Shawn's 2006 deployment was adult women. Because of their religious prohibitions, women had no contact with American males.

THIRD DEPLOYMENT—2009

It was on this deployment that I noticed the biggest change in the interaction between Americans and Iraqis—and it was rewarding. In the five years since I first went to Iraq, a lot had changed. In 2004, we were there for combat. In 2009, I was a member of a thirteen-man team working to train the Iraqi police, with thirteen of us interacting with Iraqi police officers every single day. We often spent a full day with them on missions, as well as training them on how to use firearms, conduct police investigations, and control people in tense situations. What made it even more rewarding is that the United States included some actual U.S. police officers on the team to help with fingerprinting, investigative techniques, and so forth. We really came to enjoy our interactions with our Iraqi counterparts."

In fact, with earlier barriers down, Shawn found the Iraqis to be a very cordial and friendly people. "In the U.S., we shake hands. In Iraq, you hug. While it took time and patience to build trust, eventually we became friends. The language was always a barrier, but much of what we do doesn't require language."

Shawn's unit worked particularly hard to gain the trust of tribal leaders: "We knew we were on the right track when these leaders invited us into their homes to share meals not just with the men, but with the whole family. I have warm memories of sitting in their living rooms with their large family eating a feast of a dinner."

The Americans knew that this was a sacrifice on the part of the Iraqis because they had little money, even the leaders. "To be in the same room sharing a meal with their wife, children, and in-laws was a huge sign of respect and friendship on their part."

But it wasn't easy for either side. Opponents of the new government wanted to disrupt the daily lives of the Iraqi people. They did so by destroying their schools, their police stations, and hurting or killing those who cooperated with the new government.

> Because the Iraqi police were working directly with us, they often became targets. In an attempt to provide security and stability for their neighborhoods, they put themselves directly in the line of fire. It was very hard on them emotionally because they could be targeted at any time, both on the job and later at home.

A disturbing incident occurred after Shawn's group left one area:

> A general with whom we had formed a trusted relationship, and who had invited us into his home, became a target. One day, a short time after we left, insurgents drove a suicide vehicle loaded with an IED (improvised explosive device) into the general's house, blowing it up. Many members of his family were injured, and some killed.

Nonetheless, strong bonds of brotherhood were developed with local police, and the Marines found it gratifying to share their knowledge and training with friends.

OPERATION EAGLE SCOUT PROJECT

Naturally, Shawn shared these experiences with his family in letters, satellite phone calls, and emails. When his younger brother, Cameron McKinnon, was sixteen years old he needed to come up with a service project to earn the rank of Eagle Scout in the Boy

Scouts of America. "Cameron decided that he wanted to do something for the people in Iraq I'd been telling him about."

After his proposal was accepted, Cameron and his family, as well as other Scouts in his troop, started to raise money to buy school supplies and clothing for children in Iraq. They cleaned cars at their church. At a cost of $3 to vacuum and clean out their cars, lots of people showed up to make a donation. With the proceeds of their work, the Scouts purchased more than 300 pounds of goods to ship to Iraq in twelve large boxes.

"The war had gone on for so long," says Shawn, "that the clothing of most of Iraqi children was in tatters. They had to wear the same clothes every day, and their parents simply didn't have the money to buy new clothes. That's why Cameron's project was so meaningful and helpful in our efforts to build trust in the local community."

One of the first places Shawn and his team went to deliver clothing was to a woman's shelter for those whose husbands had been killed in combat:

> The adults wouldn't wear the clothing because it was not traditional. But it was okay for the kids to wear American-style clothes. The children didn't have anything in the way of school supplies—the local government built very austere concrete buildings for schools, but there was no money for supplies. So, we had a great time handing out school supplies like pencils, paper, and crayons. The kids loved it.

Shawn and his group gave leftover supplies to the children of the Iraqi police officers with whom they worked:

> They knew about the project because we started bringing packages with us to work. Our interpreter was from Baghdad, and he explained to them why we

were giving out these gifts—that it was a gift from my brother and his friends in America. That made a deep impression on the Iraqis and helped them understand that Marines have families back home. Knowing that we had that in common strengthened our bond.

They were also able to use the supplies when tribal chiefs came to meet with their U.S. liaisons. Shawn's team set up security, and while he was on duty, a few children approached them out of curiosity.

It was great that we could pass things out to them. I remember that just a few had the courage to come up initially, but when we started passing out school supplies and clothes the rest of the children just swarmed us, hoping to get something that was new and that could be uniquely theirs. Of course this had an impact on the way the adult leaders thought about us.

All in all we were able to give things to several hundred children. I was happy to do that for any child, but it had the most meaning giving to the police officers with whom we worked. We saw them every day, and they were so grateful for the items we gave to them and their families. It meant a lot to all of us.

Shawn continued:

One of the Iraqis we had the greatest affection for was a fellow we nicknamed Roger. A lot of our supplies went to his family. Roger was a big, heavy-set guy who was always happy. We had lunch with him frequently, sometimes with his family. They made a drink called *Chi*, which is a warm, sugary sweet drink that comes in a one-ounce glass.

When asked why this fellow was called Roger, Shawn laughed.

> It's because he heard us say the word *Roger* to con-
> firm an answer when talking with someone on our
> military radios. It was the only English word he knew
> how to say. Sometimes he'd walk up to our radios and
> randomly push a button and say, "Roger." It was his
> way of establishing contact. So, we gave him the nick-
> name Roger.

Becoming serious, Shawn reports that Roger was later wounded by insurgents, likely because he was friendly to the Americans.

HUMAN FACE—HUMAN FRIENDS

Three hundred pounds of clothing and school supplies don't go all that far in a country of 38 million people. But to an Iraqi child who has nothing, a new shirt or pair of pants or a notebook and pencils means everything. And to their parents, who struggle every day to put food on the table amidst the violence of their society, it means the world. In this small way, Shawn and all the other Americans who treat the Iraqis with respect are ambassadors of goodwill. Combining that respect with an Eagle Scout project from a younger brother is a recipe for showing humanity in the aftermath of war.

TODAY

Shawn McKinnon's service in the Marine Corps came to an end, and he returned to the United States. He married and started a family. Today, he is a police officer in Kaysville, Utah, where he uses many of the techniques he shared with the police officers in Iraq. Recognizing the value of connecting with his community, he reaches out to city leaders and schools and has built strong bonds of respect for the men and women he works with every day. In short, his experience in Iraq has a direct bearing on his lifetime profession. It's hard to imagine anyone being better at police work than Shawn. He is at once both gentle and strong, representing what is best in the men and women who serve in uniform, whether at home or abroad.

CHAPTER 15

CHARLES AND DONNA COOLEY
THE HAPPY FACTORY

Bill, a young American soldier serving in Iraq, wrote home to his aunt and uncle:

> Please reassure the folks that make the toys at the Happy Factory that they make a huge, huge, difference in the comfort of Iraqi children.

Bill's aunt and uncle passed along his message and story to Charles and Donna Cooley:

> Our nephew who is serving in Iraq shared a very touching story.
> The last patrol they were on, they investigated a safe house used by the enemy. It had been destroyed by

the enemy before they left. The insurgents left behind a mother and her young son in the rubble, both with terrible wounds. Our nephew Bill said that the little boy had most of his cheek and jaw missing. He said what was eerie was that the child never cried but just looked terrified. So, while they waited for the medics, Bill gave this little boy the last toy he had with him. He said for as much as this suffering child could move his face, Bill knew he was smiling. He kept hugging Bill and wouldn't let him go, even when the medics arrived. Bill said the little fellow just clutched the toy to his chest. Other than the tattered clothes on his back, Bill was pretty sure this was the only possession this child had. So, Bill passes on a thousand thank yous to the "toy people."[1]

This is one of innumerable emails and thank-you letters received by the volunteers at the Happy Factory in the small, southern Utah community of Cedar City. In this case, Bill's aunt and uncle had given him sixty wooden toys from the Happy Factory before he was deployed to Iraq. So this email details only one of sixty incidents of making a child happy—but perhaps it is the most poignant: It shows how a single toy can make a huge difference in the life of a child in terror or pain.

Today, Happy Factory has placed more than 1.5 million toys in the hands of children in 180 countries around the world. But it didn't start out with such grand ambitions. Rather, it was the effort of a one married couple to make handmade wooden toys to give to local children in distress. It has now evolved into an all-volunteer production team with an ever-increasing reach. Many of the toys created by the Happy Factory have found their way into war zones where they help American soldiers connect with local people and feel the joy of lighting up a child's life. That is therapeutic for both the child and the soldier.

The Happy Factory's most elaborate toy, a large wooden steam shovel on which a child can sit and manipulate the bucket, has proved an incredible blessing to seriously disabled children. Somehow, playing with the steam shovel unlocks the minds of these children and has led to what some of the people who work with the children call "steam shovel therapy." It's as if a light had suddenly turned on in darkened little brains with the power to "help rejuvenate minds."[2]

Perhaps most incredible of all is that no Happy Factory worker receives any compensation whatsoever. "The Happy Factory is a 501(c)(3) qualifying non-profit organization whose sole mission is to give the children of the world a small, high-quality, wooden toy, so every child has at least one toy. We are made up of volunteers, have no payroll, and none of the Board of Directors are paid, so 100% of every dollar donated is used in the production of our toys."[3]

This is a story about mercy magnified. From small beginnings to a remarkable impact all around the world, it touches on how people have been blessed both in war and in individual medical adversity. The people at the Happy Factory have shown that one does not have to physically be in other parts of the world to extend mercy and love to others.

SIMPLE BEGINNINGS

Charles and Donna Cooley retired from Southern Utah University in 1995, having spent their careers working with young people. Donna was the school's bursar (head cashier) for most of those years. Her husband, "Charlie," ran the university's sports and cultural arena, the 5,400 seat Centrum. When they retired, Charles tinkered with his woodworking equipment and found pleasure in creating small animal cutouts. Donna hand-painted the cutouts.

Because supply quickly exceeded demand in their own family,

Charles took plenty of toys when he and Donna visited Primary Children's Medical Center in Salt Lake City, 250 miles north of Cedar City. She was taking blankets made by her church's women's group to donate to the hospital. But the toys were a huge hit with the small patients who suffered from cancer, burns, and other maladies that required extended hospitalization. "We got more hugs there than we did at a family reunion," said Charles.[4] That inspired him to make more toys and has led to monthly deliveries since that first excursion in 1995.

Feeling good about what they'd accomplished, Charles and Donna donated additional toys to groups in the Cedar City area. The best part, of course, was seeing children playing with their toys, experiencing priceless joy because of their simple gift.

With a growing appreciation of the profound effect their toys were having in children's lives, Charles started creating small cars and trucks that added motion to the toys. Perhaps the most popular was called a flapper. The kids loved them. Donna painted as fast as she could as ever more requests came their way.

Then on one of their trips to Salt Lake City, they stopped by the Shriner's Children Hospital with a box of toys. The toys proved of great value in distracting children from their pain. But when they talked with hospital administrators, they learned that Shriner's already had access to commercially produced toys. What they needed were specialty wood items to help the children maneuver. Shriner's hospitals treat children with bone, muscle, and joint problems. "We had unique needs and I was always looking for resources," said Lisa Carter, a physical therapist at Shriner's. "When I called Charles and asked if he could make us wedge boards that assist children to stretch and strengthen tight or weak muscles, he said, 'Sure. Just send us the plans.'"

These uniquely created items included a transfer board that allowed a child with muscular dystrophy to be moved from his wheelchair to his bed without his mother having to physically lift him. Donna and Charles's efforts also provided a wooden tray–easel combination that allowed a sixteen-year-old girl confined to a wheelchair by cerebral palsy and spastic paralysis to write without the pain of bending forward. Thus the Cooleys started making wooden items that were either too expensive commercially or simply unavailable.[5]

The project went worldwide when the Cooleys donated some toys to LDS Humanitarian Services, which distributes aid as part of relief efforts following a natural disaster. The response to the Cooleys' toys was the same wherever they were sent—children loved them and found great solace in having a possession that was uniquely theirs.

THE FOUNDATION: NEW BEGINNINGS

While cutting out toys early one morning—Donna is known to start her work at the factory as early as four o'clock—Charles found himself thinking about the smiles of the children that received the toys. Those images inspired him. *The Happy Factory,* he thought. *We are a Happy Factory.* And that's how the project got its name.

In time, word got out in Cedar City about the important work being done by the Cooleys, and neighbors and strangers offered to help. Their small, two-person operation had to be enlarged if it was to have both a broader reach and continuity across time. Somehow resources became available just as they were needed. For example, in early 1999 Charles was introduced to David Grant, president of the Cedar City–based Metalcraft Technologies that manufactures custom sheets for the aerospace industry. After seeing the tiny shed where Charles and two other workers cut out toys, David went to his board of directors. In addition to a $5,000 donation, they offered the Happy Factory space in their large manufacturing building. The Cooleys were overwhelmed. Metalcraft Technologies refitted one entire section with the appropriate wiring and exhaust systems so the operation could expand.[6]

After the expansion, it seemed that everyone wanted toys from the Happy Factory. Hundreds of people, from high school students to long-retired seniors, wanted to volunteer. Soon, Happy Factory was sending wooden toys to distressed children in "hospitals, family shelters, churches, schools, Native American organizations, foundations, medical clinics, crisis centers, Head Start centers, orphanages, and to victims of natural disasters."[7] Volunteers going to such places often carry toys with them to give directly to the children.

From a strictly logical point of view, their ultimate goal of getting a toy into the hands of every needy child in the world is impossible. With billions of children living in poverty, in war zones, or at the site of natural disasters, the Cooleys and their fellow volunteers simply can't reach everyone. But as someone told Charles, "One toy may be only a drop in the bucket of the world's needs, but it's a big drop for the child who gets it." Donna Cooley says this simple phrase changed the way they thought about their project and inspired them to make it as big as they could. It changed what they did from a hobby into a full-time labor of love. Now their motto is, "We may not be able to make a toy for every child in the world who needs one, but we're going to try."

IRAQ AND AFGHANISTAN

People who are interested in distributing the toys often stop by the Happy Factory before going to troubled places in the world. Large organizations, such as Doctors Without Borders, pay to have toys shipped so their physicians can distribute them while performing medical procedures on children in remote locations. Some area shipping companies send the toys free to redistribution points. But when it came to the wars in the Middle East, it fell to the members of the military serving there to hand deliver the toys. Often family members pick up the toys and send them to their soldier in the field for redistribution. "It's hard to say how many toys have found their way to Iraq and Afghanistan," says Donna Cooley. "But we know that many have, and that they make a real difference to the children who receive them."

Perhaps the most startling story of all came in the form of a phone call from a young man serving in Iraq. Fred Anderson told it to Ed Ebert, both of whom are Happy Factory volunteers in St. George, Utah. The story shows how the simple wooden toys from Utah saved the lives of some U.S. servicemen in Iraq. Here is how Fred related the story to Ed:

> I received a phone call from my grandson who is serving in Iraq. He said that shortly after they left their base a few days earlier they encountered a little girl sitting in the middle of the road. She wouldn't move at our approach, so we got out to talk to her. She pointed to a spot in the road where the dirt had been disturbed. When we checked it out we found that a landmine had been placed there. This allowed us to remove it safely before it hurt anyone. It turns out that the little girl had watched some insurgents place it there the night before and she knew that it was intended to hurt Americans. While she was talking with us she was holding a Happy Factory toy tightly in her hands. She said that the Americans had given her the toy and so she liked the Americans and didn't want them to get hurt. That's why she was sitting in the middle of the road to warn us.[8]

The young soldier said, "It was a toy just like the ones you make, Grandpa." That is how many lives were blessed by the efforts of the hundreds of volunteers, including Fred Anderson, who work in the Happy Factory every week.

CHARLES COOLEY, 1930–2011

> There are many things that I cannot do. There are
> many things I do not know. But there is one thing I
> can do: I can serve another. I don't need any praise,
> notoriety, or pay because the satisfaction, blessings,
> and feelings that I receive are so great that I need noth-
> ing else.—Charles Cooley

From 1995 until his death in 2011, Charles Cooley was a driving force behind the good work of the Happy Factory. Since her husband's death, Donna continues to spend nearly every day working in behalf of the cause they created twenty years earlier.

Today, the factory operates under the direction of Douglas Carr, a retired engineer who spent his career designing wind tunnels. Doug sees a parallel in the work he now does as general manager in organizing the processes that allow the factory to produce more than 4,000 toys per week, using hundreds of volunteers from Southern Utah University, retired people (some of whom come in every single day), and anyone who can spare a little time to brighten the world.

Charles and Donna Cooley created a legacy and set an example for others to follow. Time and a little effort can spread joy to children all over the world.

AUTHOR'S NOTE

On a recent trip to Europe, my wife and I toured Paris. As we gazed at the Eiffel Tower, visited the gardens of the Tuileries near the Place de la Concorde ("Place of Harmony"), and marveled at the wonderful museums, I realized that all of it would have been destroyed if Adolf Hitler had had his way. In his selfish fury, he wanted only to destroy. But Hitler did not realize his dream of destruction because brave men and women rose up to save Paris, including General Dietrich von Choltitz, Raoul Nordling, and other thoughtful persons. These men and women risked their lives to save history, and their legacy will last for generations. More important, as I looked around at the crowds of young Parisians enjoying a late August afternoon, I wondered how many would never have been born if the German occupiers had followed orders in 1944 to launch the V-Rockets to kill their grandparents. The compassionate actions of disillusioned German officers during nineteen days towards the end of World War II reverberates through the years.

That's what makes the stories in this collection so meaningful—small actions by brave and compassionate individuals can have a profound effect on future lives. The passage of time magnifies the impact of their generosity. Who can say what the world would be like today if Patrick Ferguson had shot and killed George Washington? Would the Vietnam War have turned out differently if the photo of young Kim Phuc fleeing in terror and pain had never been published? And how many children have been comforted by toys made by the volunteers at the Happy Factory?

Each of the people in these stories pledged a portion of their lives to help save or comfort another person. They are heroic because they paired courage with compassion and mercy. I hope you have found their examples as inspiring as I have.

NOTES

CHAPTER 1: CAPTAIN FERGUSON AND GENERAL WASHINGTON

1. Guerrilla warfare is the use of unconventional tactics by small groups of soldiers who engage the enemy from concealed positions. *Guerrilla* is derived from the Spanish *guerra*, "war," and *illa*, "little."
2. Ricky Roberts and Bryan Brown, *Every Insult & Indignity: The Life, Genius & Legacy of Major Patrick Ferguson* (CreateSpace Independent Publishing Platform, 2011), 33–34.
3. Roberts and Brown, *Every Insult & Indignity*, Kindle locations 352–59.
4. Dictated account, Jan. 31, 1778, in Roberts and Brown, *Every Insult & Indignity*, Kindle locations 1873–1876.
5. M. M. Gilchrist, "Patrick Ferguson," Independence Hall Association (1999), ushistory.org.
6. Lyman C. Draper, Anthony Allaire, and Isaac Shelby, *King's Mountain and Its Heroes: History of the Battle of King's Mountain* (Cincinnati, OH: Peter G. Thompson, 1881), 60.

CHAPTER 2: RICHARD KIRKLAND

1. James K. Bryant II, *The Battle of Fredericksburg: We Cannot Escape History* (Charleston, S.C.: The History Press, 2012), 154.
2. Joshua Chamberlain, in Bryant, *Battle of Fredericksburg*, 154–55.
3. "Richard Kirkland, the Humane Hero of Fredericksburg," Civil War Trust, quoting *Southern Historical Society Papers* (Richmond, Va.: Southern Historical Society, 1880), 8:4, civilwar.org; paragraphing altered.
4. Chester B. Goolrick, "The Angel of Marye's Heights," *Coronet*, Jan. 1957, 154, unz.org.

CHAPTER 3: THE KAISER AND ROBERT CAMPBELL

1. *Kaiser,* meaning "emperor, king," is derived from *Caesar,* the Roman imperial title used from the time of Caesar Augustus onward. *Tsar,* the Russian form of *Caesar,* also has the same meaning. Wilhelm II was crowned king of Prussia (the most powerful of the German duchies) and emperor of Germany.

2. *Germania* was the Roman name for the area that is now modern Germany.

3. This remarkable story was found by British historian Richard van Emden while doing research for his book *Meeting the Enemy: The Human Face of War* (New York: Bloomsbury, 2013).

4. "Revealed: Extraordinary Story of British WWI Captain Released by Kaiser," dailymail.com.

5. "Revealed: Extraordinary Story of British WWI Captain Released by Kaiser," dailymail.com.

6. "Revealed: Extraordinary Story of British WWI Captain Released by Kaiser," dailymail.com.

CHAPTER 4: EDITH CAVELL

1. Alexandra was the wife of Edward VII of Great Britain. Born Alexandra of Denmark, she became queen-empress consort when her husband became king of the United Kingdom and Ireland and emperor of India at the death of Queen Victoria in 1901.

2. Jack Batten, *Silent in an Evil Time: The Brave War of Edith Cavell* (Toronto: Tundra Books, 2007), 11.

3. Brunel was a famous engineer and inventor in the nineteenth century. He designed the Great Western Railway, which connected London with the Midlands and Wales, as well as ocean-going steamships. His ship, the *Great Britain,* is considered the first modern steamship. Built of metal, it used a propeller rather than paddlewheels for propulsion and coal-fired engines instead of sails as the exclusive source of power for ocean crossings.

4. Batten, *Silent in an Evil Time,* 33–34.

5. WWI casualty and death tables, U.S. Department of Justice, pbs.org /greatwar.

6. Joy LaValley, "Edith Cavell," *Relevance: The Quarterly Journal of the Great War Society* 5, no. 1, worldwar1.com.

7. Batten, *Silent in an Evil Time*, 70–72.
8. Batten, *Silent in an Evil Time*, 83–84.
9. Batten, *Silent in an Evil Time*, 84–85.
10. Batten, *Silent in an Evil Time*, 99–100.
11. "Edith Cavell," britannica.com.
12. Batten, *Silent in an Evil Time*, 113.

CHAPTER 5: OSWALD BÖELCKE

1. Edward (Eddie) V. Rickenbacker, in Louis E. Orcutt, ed., *Supplementary Volume to the Great War History* (New York: The Christian Herald, 1920), 145.
2. Manfred Freiherr von Richthofen, *The Red Battle Flyer*, trans. J. Ellis Barker (1915), in *Richthofen & Böelcke in Their Own Words* (Leonaur Books, 2011), 67.
3. C. G. Grey, footnote to *Böelcke, Aviator's Field Book*, in *Richthofen & Böelcke in Their Own Words*, 105.
4. Oswald Böelcke, *An Aviator's Field Book*, trans. Robert Reynold Hirsch (1915), in *Richthofen & Böelcke in Their Own Words*, 144.
5. Johannes Werner, *Knight of Germany: Oswald Böelcke, German Ace* (Havertown: Casemate Publishers, 2009), 162.
6. Michael Seamark, "Gentlemen of the Skies," *Daily Mail*, Sept. 7, 2012, dailymail.co.uk.
7. Böelcke, *Aviator's Field Book*, in *Richthofen & Böelcke in Their Own Words*, 175–76.
8. Theodore Roosevelt, in Henry Bordeaux, *Georges Guynemer: Knight of the Air*, trans. Louise Morgan Sill (New Haven, Conn.: Yale University Press, 1918), 11.
9. "On Being a Warrior," *Newsweek*, Apr. 13, 1997.
10. Churchill, in "Great Aviation quotes," skygod.com.

CHAPTER 6: EDITH WHARTON

1. Shari Benstock, *No Gifts from Chance: A Biography of Edith Wharton* (New York: Scribner's, 1994), 26.
2. Edith Wharton, *A Backward Glance*, annotated ed. (Moorside Press, 2013), 14.
3. Wharton, *Backward Glance*, 29–30.
4. Kay Davis, *Class and Leisure at America's First Resort, Newport Rhode*

Island, 1870–1914 (Charlottesville: University of Virginia, 2001), xroads.virginia.edu.

5. Davis, *Class and Leisure at America's First Resort,* 365.

6. Wharton, *Backward Glance,* 364–67.

7. Wharton, *Backward Glance,* 376.

8. Wharton, *Backward Glance,* 377.

9. Wharton, *Fighting France: From Dunkerque to Belfort* (1915, repr. 2012), Kindle location 416–21.

10. Wharton, *Fighting France,* Kindle location 416–21.

11. Wharton, *Backward Glance,* 386–87.

CHAPTER 7: HERR ROSENAU AND ALEX LURYE

1. The town is identified as Seldes, Germany, in Nathan Yisrael, "The Kindness That Came Back," *Jewish Magazine,* Nov. 1997, jewishmag .com. A thorough internet search, however, uncovered no German town of that name. Although the spelling of *Seldes* ends in an *s,* the word is pronounced *Selden* when used as a family name. There is a town of Selden in eastern Germany, but the Allies did not advance that far before the Armistice was declared. These facts suggest that the actual name of the town in which Alex Lurye had this experience is not preserved in the written record.

CHAPTER 8: RUDOLF WOBBE

1. Interview with Rudi Wobbe; see Rudi Wobbe and Jerry Borrowman, *Three against Hitler* (American Fork, Utah: Covenant Communications, 2002), 5–6.

2. Interview with Rudi Wobbe; see Wobbe and Borrowman, *Three against Hitler,* 28–29.

3. Interview with Rudi Wobbe; see Wobbe and Borrowman, *Three against Hitler,* 76.

4. Interview with Rudi Wobbe; see Wobbe and Borrowman, *Three against Hitler,* 79.

5. Interview with Rudi Wobbe; see Wobbe and Borrowman, *Three against Hitler,* 83.

6. Interview with Rudi Wobbe; see Wobbe and Borrowman, *Three against Hitler,* 128.

7. Interview with Rudi Wobbe; see Wobbe and Borrowman, *Three against Hitler,* 129.

8. Interview with Rudi Wobbe; see Wobbe and Borrowman, *Three against Hitler,* 130.

CHAPTER 9: DIETRICH VON CHOLTITZ

1. Larry Collins and Dominique Lapierre, *Is Paris Burning?* (1964; repr., 2000), Kindle locations 806–16.
2. Collins and Lapierre, *Is Paris Burning?* Kindle location 1414.
3. Collins and Lapierre, *Is Paris Burning?* Kindle locations 1447–60.
4. Kelly Bell, "Dietrich von Choltitz: Saved Paris from Destruction During World War II," historynet.com.
5. Collins, and Lapierre, *Is Paris Burning?* Kindle locations 3183–3197.
6. Collins and Lapierre, *Is Paris Burning?* Kindle locations 3568—3574.

CHAPTER 10: ROBERT SHEEKS

1. Gerald A. Meehl, *One Marine's War* (Annapolis, Md.: Naval Institute Press, 2012), 31–32.
2. Meehl, *One Marine's War,* 88–89. See also Harold J. Goldberg, *D-Day in the Pacific: The Battle of Saipan* (Bloomington: Indiana Univ. Press, 2007), 190.
3. Meehl, *One Marine's War,* 44–47.
4. Meehl, *One Marine's War,* 88–89.
5. Meehl, *One Marine's War,* 143.
6. Meehl, *One Marine's War,* 157.
7. Meehl, *One Marine's War,* 160–61.
8. Meehl, *One Marine's War,* 165.
9. Meehl, *One Marine's War,* 171–72.
10. Meehl, *One Marine's War,* 174.
11. Meehl, *One Marine's War,* 173.
12. See www.robertbsheeks.com.

CHAPTER 11: BERNIE FISHER

1. Interviews with Colonel Bernard Fisher, USAF, Medal of Honor. See Bernard Fisher and Jerry Borrowman, *Beyond the Call of Duty* (Salt Lake City: Shadow Mountain, 2004).
2. Each squadron had its own call sign. I was assigned "Hobo" while one of our companion squadrons was "Surf." Rescue missions were identified as a "Sandy." The call sign reduced the risk of misunderstanding when communicating by radio.

3. T. R. Sturm, *Airman,* Mar. 1967, 5.

4. After his aircraft erupted in flames, Jump stripped off his parachute, gun, helmet, and survival gear before attempting to get out of the cockpit and run to safety.

CHAPTER 12: KIM PHUC

1. President Nixon realized the powerful effect the photo had on public opinion and speculated that it must have been doctored to increase the effect. That did not happen—the photo was taken in real time as little Kim Phuc, in unimaginable pain, fled the temple where she had sheltered.

2. Denise Chong, *The Girl in the Picture: The Story of Kim Phuc, the Photograph, and the Vietnam War* (London: Penguin Books, 2001), 68.

3. Chong, *Girl in the Picture,* 76–79.

4. Chong, *Girl in the Picture,* 86.

5. "Kim's Story," Kim Phuc Foundation International, kimfoundation. com.

6. Chong, *Girl in the Picture,* 96–97.

7. "Background," Kim Phuc Foundation International, kimfoundation. com.

8. Chong, *Girl in the Picture,* 363.

9. Alina Machado, "Kim Phuc, Who Was Girl from Iconic Vietnam Photo, Begins New Treatment," cnn.com.

10. Yanan Wang, "Forty-three Years After the Burns That Made Her the 'Napalm Girl,' Kim Phuc Gets Treatment for Scars," *Washington Post,* Oct. 26, 2015, washingtonpost.com.

11. Wang, "Forty-three Years."

CHAPTER 13: HUNTER SCOTT

1. Doug Stanton, *In Harm's Way: The Sinking of the USS Indianapolis and the Extraordinary Story of Its Survivors* (New York: Henry Holt), Kindle locations 544–49.

2. Peter Nelson, *Left for Dead* (New York: Random House), Kindle location 355–60.

3. Stanton, *In Harm's Way,* Kindle locations 2273–78; paragraphing altered.

4. Nelson, *Left for Dead,* Kindle location 1830.

5. Nelson, *Left for Dead,* Kindle location 3063.

6. Nelson, *Left for Dead,* Kindle location 3112.

7. U.S. Senate Armed Services Committee hearing report, *The Sinking of the USS Indianapolis and the Subsequent Court-martial of Rear Admiral Charles B. McVay III,* 1st session, 106th Congress, Sept. 14, 1999.

8. Janis Magin, "Navy Exonerates WWII Captain," *Argus-Press,* July 13, 2001.

CHAPTER 14: SHAWN MCKINNON

1. Pub. L. 107–243 <http://legislink.org/us/pl-107–243> 116 Stat. 1498 <http://legislink.org/us/stat-116–1498> Extracted 11/25/2015.

2. "Joint Resolution to Authorize the Use of United States Armed Forces against Iraq," press release, Oct. 2, 2002.

3. This quotation and all others from Shawn McKinnon are from the author's interviews with him.

CHAPTER 15: CHARLES AND DONNA COOLEY

1. Donna Cooley, e-mail, Nov. 28, 2015.

2. happyfactory.org.

3. happyfactory.org.

4. happyfactory.org.

5. Mack Chrysler, *The Happy Factory* (Salt Lake City: KMC Publishing, 2005), 22–23.

6. Chrysler, *Happy Factory,* 30–31.

7. happyfactory.org.

8. Donna Cooley, notes about the phone call she received from Ed Ebert, St. George, Utah, relating his conversation with Fred Anderson.

INDEX

IMAGE CREDITS

All images are used by permission.

Page 5: Ferguson's Corps of British Riflemen 1777, 2015 (w/c & gouache on paper), Don Troiani (b.1949)/Private Collection/Bridgeman Images.

Page 13: © Carolyn M. Carpenter/Shutterstock.com; statue: Angel of Marye's Heights, CSA Sgt. Richard Kirkland, Battle of Fredericksburg, December 1862.

Page 23: Ak Kaiser Wilhelm II von Preußen, Orden, Bruststern, Junge jahre (b/w photo), German Photographer/Private Collection/© Arkivi UG. All Rights Reserved/Bridgeman Images.

Page 31: British nurse Edith Louisa Cavell (1865–1915), Library of Congress, Prints and Photographs Division, Washington, D.C. LC-B2- 3652-1, Bain Collection.

Page 43: Oswald Böelcke (1891–1916), Library of Congress Prints and Photographs Division Washington, D.C. LC-B2-3756-3, Bain Collection.

Page 50: Edith Wharton, Library of Congress, Prints and Photographs Division, Washington, D.C. LC-USZ62-29408.

Page 61: Jewish badges, © Yakov Oskanov/Shutterstock.com.

Page 67: Concentration camp at Auschwitz Birkenau KZ Poland © Christoph Lischetzki/Shutterstock.com.

Page 79: Eiffel Tower, Paris, France, Library of Congress, Prints and Photographs Division, Washington, D.C. LC-H2-B-11068, Harris & Ewing Collection.

Page 93: Japan's Naval Ensign, © nazlisart/Shutterstock.com.

Page 108: Bernard Fisher and Jump Myers after rescue, Air Force photograph.

Page 126: Hanoi, Vietnam, flag on tower, © v.schlichting/Shutterstock.com.

Page 143: *USS Indianapolis* (CA-35), Off the Mare Island Navy Yard, California, 10 July 1945, after her final overhaul and repair of combat damage. Photograph from the Bureau of Ships Collection, U.S. National Archives. Catalog no.: 19-N-86911.

Page 160: Silhouettes of military soldiers, © BPTU/Shutterstock.com.

Page 175: Charles and Donna Cooley, photograph by Ken Bonzo.